5/96

W H I T E W A T E R
RAFTING
AN INTRODUCTORY GUIDE

16

WHITEWATER
RAFTING
AN INTRODUCTORY GUIDE

~~~~~~~~

C E C I L   K U H N E

Lyons & Burford,
Publishers

Printed in the United States of America
Illustrations © by Manuel F. Cheo
Text design by Rohani Design, Edmonds, WA.

10 9 8 7 6 5 4 3 2 1

Library of Congress Cataloging-in-Publication Data

Kuhne, Cecil, 1952–
    Whitewater rafting: an introductory guide / Cecil Kuhne.
        p.   cm.
    Includes index.
    ISBN 1-55821-317-1
    1. Rafting (Sports) 2. Rafting (Sports)--Equipment and supplies.
    3. Rivers--United States--Guidebooks.   I. Title.
GV780.K836 1995
796.1'22--dc20   94-41146
                                                               CIP

For Ma Chérie

CONTENTS

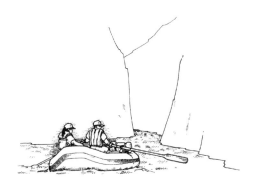

CHAPTER 1

RIVER FEVER

It was one of those rare and glorious summer days along the most beautiful river I had ever seen. Life seemed deliciously complete and full of hope. The immense river reflected the broad, sullen clouds which hovered above as the light danced off its swirling surface.

Our group of twelve ordinary mortals was perched nervously several hundred feet above the moving water so punctuated with rapids that it looked intimidating, even from that distance. "See that rapid?" asked our guide, Mike Hipsher, with a sly grin. "That's Milky Way. It's a monster. We'll be lucky if we don't flip the raft."

The rapid itself was rimmed with somber, glistening rock. Instinctively, our eyes moved downstream—to the mass of jumbled crosscurrents, recirculating holes, and nasty sharp waves churning below. I could feel the inside of my stomach start to tighten.

The guides called the process "reading" whitewater: the art that experienced boaters practice to evaluate a stretch of rapids to determine which route through the boulders and waves will provide the least amount of damage to gear—and themselves.

We spent a lot of time that afternoon sizing up Milky Way from the shore, trying to figure out where the current would take us. We talked excitedly among ourselves, pointing to obstructions in the river and occasionally throwing a piece of driftwood into the current to determine its flow.

Over the roar of the rapids, questions kept racing through my mind. Could each of the rapids be run? If so, would we emerge in the right position to enter the next one? Could we remember all the hazards through the obstacle course?

Mike asked for a show of hands from those who wanted to run the rapids. It looked so intimidating that many in the group decided to walk around the enormous pounding waves rather than navigate them.

Those who decided not to board the rafts said little, but shuffled their feet nervously and stared into the whitewater void below. I could see the fear in their faces—and in my throat I could taste my own. I couldn't decide whether or not to run the rapid.

Boulders of all sizes lay across three-fourths of the river's width, forcing the flow against the steep cliff on the left. Rocks had clogged the channel, but the river had fingered its way through, leaving chutes of various widths, most of which were too narrow to be considered.

"Look at that huge suction hole caused by those submerged rocks," Mike cautioned as he pointed downstream. "But there's a narrow little tongue of smooth water between them. See it? That's where we need to be if we're going to make it."

"But the right side has a pretty steep hole." I tried to appear calm. "What happens if we miss it and go in there?"

Mike paused, and then leaned slightly forward. "Maybe we had better aim for the left side. The water's moving through it much better. If we get dumped, at least we'll be washed through." I could feel my heart racing, and I tried to think of reasons why I couldn't go along.

The guides and their crews of volunteers began to run the rafts through, one at a time. Each boat barely survived without tipping over, until only one was left. I looked around for Mike, the last guide. Suddenly I felt a hand on my shoulder. "Let's go," he said. I opened my mouth to say something, but nothing came out.

Five of us walked back to the boat and climbed in for the inevitable descent. I coiled the bowline while Mike fussed nervously with the straps on his life jacket. My mouth had become as dry as the beach we were standing on, and I wished I had told Mike that his group would have to go without me.

We paddled into the glistening current. The two huge boulders at the top of the rapid were located easily. We entered them, but the fury downriver was still out of sight. As the white froth of the rapids neared, the force of the current swiftly pulled the raft downstream. For a moment, in the slack water above the rapids, the boat hung suspended.

With his booming voice, Mike directed the powerful strokes necessary for us to shuttle from one side of the river to the other. "The hole is right there . . . paddle hard to the left . . . watch out for that rock . . . go for the tongue just ahead!" By following his commands, we were able—but only barely—to avoid the dark, gaping holes which seemed bottomless. Why had I agreed to this madness?

Then, with the speed of a roller coaster, the raft entered the sleek, sharply tapered tongue—a sliver of smooth, green silk unfurled before the churning whitewater. We plunged downward into the watery abyss. We hit pay dirt.

We hugged the shore until we passed the huge boulder in mid-stream. The worry I felt was slowly giving way to confidence that we were going to make it. But then I saw, directly ahead, a series of massive waves.

Like an errant piece of flotsam in a whirlpool, the raft rocked uncontrollably from side to side as it flashed past the huge swells of the cataclysm. We were plastered by its wall of water, and we grabbed onto whatever handhold we could find to keep from being washed into the rocky depths.

A wave of tremendous force rolled across the bow of the boat. When we opened our eyes again, we saw that one of our crew had been swept overboard, where he bobbed next to the raft, his head barely above water. "Grab him by the life jacket!" Mike screamed. Several of us leaned precariously over the tube and pulled him in as he gasped for air.

The remaining seconds seemed like hours before we hit calm water. Amazingly enough, we had endured the intense pounding unscathed. Only a couple of hats and a pair of sunglasses had been lost overboard.

We all jumped up, screaming with joy at our success. The gray clouds hanging overhead had disappeared, giving way to brilliant sunshine. It was my first trip down the rapids. I was hooked.

The beauty of all this, of course, is that the entire country is filled with rapids just like Milky Way. There is, however, one caveat should you choose to try your luck. In the process, you will most likely develop an incurable case of river fever—which means that before the trip is over, you'll be planning the next one.

There is a story often told about a rafting party about to depart on a clear, rushing stream in Colorado. A small group was seeing them off. Naturally, the event attracted the attention of passersby, and before long, a crowd gathered. One observer, a middle-aged bank employee, watched the scene from a bridge overhead.

The rafters said their final farewells and began to paddle away from the shore. Just as the rafts entered the current, the banker—incapable of restraining himself any longer—tore off his coat and tie and jumped into the river. He swam furiously toward the boat where he was pulled in by the other passengers—all to the cheers of the crowd.

The thrill of a river trip is contagious. Memories of river trips I have taken ten or fifteen years ago are so vivid in my mind it seems as if they happened last week.

There is a rapid on the Youghiogheny River in Maryland called Meat Cleaver. It calls to mind the expression, "If you ain't scared, you ain't havin' fun." This is one of the most notorious rapids on one of the East's most notorious rivers. It starts off as a bob-and-weave affair among big boulders and enormous waves. It ends dramatically with a steep ledge packed with two sharp rocks that threaten to impale anything not pointed in the right direction.

Then there is Pillow Rock Rapid on the Gauley River in West Virginia, where the river plows through 80 yards of foam and fury at a pace so swift it's difficult to comprehend. The rapid tumbles toward a huge rock the size of a house where the current churns, falls toward another rock, and finally spits boaters out with a vengeance.

On the other hand, running Hell's Kitchen, a rapid on California's Tuolumne River is an experience not unlike that of walking into an open fire hose. But what a difference the scenery makes: unspoiled wilderness, abundant wildlife, an area steeped in the folklore of Miwok Indians and early gold seekers. Only periodically do boaters escape the grip of the current and are able to take a few seconds to catch their breath and shake out their arms and hands.

Eating a solid wall of water is one of the quintessential experiences of rafting. Nowhere is this more in evidence than on Colorado's Arkansas River. The most popular raft trip is through granite-walled Brown's Canyon near Buena Vista. Huge boulders and a steep gradient create dozens of exciting rapids like the infamous Zoom Flume. Many people compare the experience to driving a convertible down an expressway during Hurricane Beulah.

On the Chattooga, the wrong choice on a rapid like Sock-em Dog is rewarded quickly with a raft draped around a rock, pinned on a log, or overturned at the base of a waterfall. But what a place: the river is framed by sheer cliffs, incredible rock formations, and the thick forests of northern Georgia and the western Carolinas. The Chattooga became famous as the location in the movie *Deliverance*. Its rapids will make a believer out of you.

You wouldn't expect whitewater in the middle of Arizona's Sonoran desert, but the Salt River has it. A number of rapids like Eye of the Needle lie in the depths of the river's Granite Gorge. The river funnels through this narrow canyon, which is sort of like trying to force Lake Superior into a drinking straw. During the spring runoff, the spectacle can be frightening—a chaos of churning whitewater that, at first glance, seems destined to swallow and hold any boat exposed to it. It's enough to make knees weaken and mouths go dry.

If you get caught sideways in a rapid like the Exterminator on Maine's Penobscot River, you'll be flipped like a leaf in a storm. The big rolling waves of this rapid move along at unbelievable speeds down a curving staircase of violent whitewater. You almost wish the river would slow down to allow more time to enjoy the incredibly beautiful Ripogenus Gorge. This is true wilderness. And this is the kind of river and rapid that confirm that life is truly an adventure for the adventurous.

Powerline Rapid is a seething cauldron churning in the depths of New Mexico's Rio Grande Gorge—a chasm so deep that the Washington Monument could be placed inside, with a hundred feet to spare. The basalt spewed up by ancient volcanoes and formed into rugged, sheer canyons is a worthy accompaniment to the plunging whitewater. One experienced boater described the run: "You aim your boat for the right place and get spit out like a watermelon seed. Hopefully right side up."

I have been very fortunate to have joined countless river journeys over the last two decades. If there's a better way to experience wilderness than floating through it on a river, I'd like to know about it. And so would the three million of us who have discovered the unsurpassable joy of paddling a raft down a deep, secluded valley on a ribbon of emerald green.

Here the forces of nature have a powerful but contradictory impact: at the same time that they quicken the pulse, they still the soul. Veteran river guide Gaylord Staveley expressed it well: "Running a river is one of the few remaining ways to compete against nature rather than against others, or against society. It's a wonderful change, a wonderful struggle, because the river lets you know immediately whether you've won or lost. In the battles of day-to-day life, one can't always recognize one's wins and losses. But the successful run of each rapid is a clear-cut victory all in itself, and the run of a whole river reiterates all of the victories along the way."

The camaraderie that often binds complete strangers on a river trip is especially memorable. Spending complete days amidst spectacular scenery, and sharing new adventures and a good meal around a campfire at the end of a day have a way of bringing people together.

Only a river trip seems to provide this inexplicable fusion of nature, water, and humanity. And that, I suppose, is why we keep coming back for more. Wallace Stegner writes in *The Sound of Mountain Water*:

> There is something ominous about a swift river and something thrilling about a river of any kind.

The nearest upstream bend is a gate out of mystery, and the nearest downstream bend a door to further mystery.

Those who hear the siren call to adventure find there is one major problem: So many rivers, so little time. But the puzzle presents one inevitable solution: a river trip!

CHAPTER 2

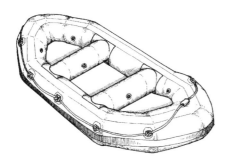

EQUIPMENT

Two developments led to the popularity of rafting as we know it today: one relating to equipment, the other to technique. A trapper named Nathaniel Galloway, from Vernal, Utah, who explored throughout the West by wooden dory, changed whitewater technique in a simple but dramatic way. Before Galloway, boatmen rowed down the river as they would on a lake. The oarsman faced upstream, without a view of the oncoming hazards downriver.

Not only did this method prevent the rower from watching the hazards downstream, but it accelerated the speed of the boat, thus increasing the dangers. Nat

Galloway changed all this in 1893. Instead of blindly rowing backward into rapids, he turned his boat around, faced downstream, and rowed against the current. This not only allowed him to see approaching rocks and holes, but greatly increased maneuverability by permitting him to slow the boat's speed downstream and to move across the width of the river to avoid obstacles.

The next development which led to rafting as a sport was related to equipment—the raft itself. During World War II, the inflatable assault raft was developed by the U.S. Navy to attack the islands of the Pacific. These black neoprene rafts, known as "ten-mans," were fifteen feet long and seven feet wide. Manufactured by the thousands, they were sold cheaply after the war as surplus. It was not long before they were running rivers throughout the West.

Compared to the wooden boats first used to float rivers, the inflatable raft was a tremendous improvement. It was more affordable, and its incredible flotation and ability to bounce off rocks unharmed made it much safer than any hard-shelled boat available. The raft was a boat whose time had come. And the sport of whitewater rafting was born.

RAFTS

No one knows for certain when it all started, but inflatable boats have been around for centuries. Pump some air into a couple of goatskins, tie them together, and you have an inflatable raft.

The modern-day inflatable, with its curvaceous lines and lightweight, high-tech, bulletproof material, replaced the heavy bulbous forms of the navy surplus rafts. Along with the quality, the costs too have vastly risen. The best model can have a price tag resembling that of a good used car. But the inflatable boat is an eminently practical and amazingly efficient piece of outdoor gear. What other boat capable of holding five people can be stuffed into a bundle not much bigger than a suitcase?

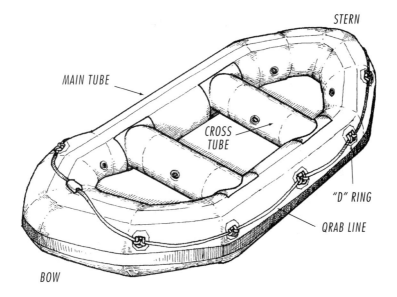

STERN

MAIN TUBE

CROSS TUBE

"D" RING

QRAB LINE

BOW

THE INFLATABLE RAFT

Compared to rigid craft, the designs of inflatable boats are relatively simple, though they have grown increasingly sophisticated over the years. With their sweeping, upturned bows and sterns, the current breed of inflatable boat is a work of art, especially considering that it's formed from nothing more than a couple of sheets of coated fabric.

Design

In general, rafts are designed to be either rowed or paddled. On a rowed raft, a single pair of oars in the hands of an experienced guide controls the boat. On a paddled raft, each person is armed with a paddle, and everyone pitches in to help control the raft. Compared to rigid craft, the designs of inflatable boats are admittedly simplistic, although they have grown increasingly sophisticated over the years. With gently sweeping, upturned bows and sterns, the current breed of inflatable boat is a work of art, especially considering that it is formed from nothing more than a couple of sheets of coated fabric.

Rafts are designed to be either symmetrical or asymmetrical. The symmetrical design allows either end of the boat to be used as bow or stern, which is especially advantageous to those who use oars, rather than paddles, because it allows the boat to be rowed either downstream in slow water or upstream in fast water. The asymmetrical design, on the other hand, is more common on boats intended for paddling, as its shortened, less-upturned stern provides a broader and more effective base from which the stern paddler can work.

Bow and stern sections of inflatable boats are shaped in either of two ways. If built with squared, compound segments, the bow and stern of the boat can be pointed, but they are more commonly blunt-nosed. (The only real variation on this theme are those rafts with tubes which diminish in size gradually toward the ends of the boat. The theory is that this design increases lift, or clearance of the tube above the water line, without increasing overall bow and stern height.) An inflatable boat's bow and stern can also be built with a rounded, sweeping curvature, but this design is more difficult to build and requires additional material.

Regardless of shape, most inflatables have upturned bows and sterns for two reasons: to ease pivoting, or turning, (a shorter waterline is created) and to decrease the spray entering the boat. (A few boaters still prefer lower bows, believing that a raft does better driving through the rapids than rising over them.) It is important, however, that the lift not be too extreme. Too much upturn allows rapids to slow or even stop the raft, and wind blowing upstream can turn the boat into a sail, making even flatwater progress a chore.

There are other design considerations: diameter of the buoyancy tubes (bigger means more flotation and stability, but less agility and, therefore, a less thrilling ride); placement of cross-tubes for best distribution of passengers and gear; location of and access to air valves; and tightness of the floor (a tight floor reduces drag but may tear more easily when passing over rocks).

Self-Bailers. Perhaps the most highly acclaimed design innovation in recent years has been the self-bailing boat. The inflatable self-bailing floor allows water to flow back into the river through grommet holes. However, the question is often presented: Are self-bailers worth the higher price and extra weight of the inflatable floor?

Bailing water out of a boat is certainly a tedious and unglamorous job, and a self-bailer not only eliminates that drudgery but by reducing the amount of water in the boat it may also improve safety. After all, a boat weighed down by gallons of water is a hard beast to maneuver and is, therefore, at greater risk of wrapping on a boulder—

Bailing out the boat.

not to mention the increased chances of tearing the bottom of a sagging floor.

There are those who stand by the conventional rafts, though, for several reasons. The self-bailing option is a more expensive one because of the additional manufacturing labor and material its inflatable floor requires (often adding 20 or 30 pounds to a boat). But the criticism most commonly inveighed against self-bailers is that the inflatable floor results in additional flotation, causing them to ride so high above the water that they have a greater tendency to flip in rapids. The other criticism sometimes leveled against self-bailers is that they are stiffer and have the tendency to surf or even slide backward in the waves of whitewater.

Finally, many boaters actually prefer water in the bottom of their rafts when they are running whitewater because the added weight in the boat helps propel the boat through the rapids. This claim has a logical basis, as long as no quick maneuvering is required.

On the other hand, many rock-studded, high-gradient rivers with Class V rapids would never have been navigated without the safety afforded by self-bailers. This is especially true with paddle rafts, when there are no extra hands available to man the bail bucket. In fact, self-bailing rafts now outnumber conventional rafts as the craft of choice for riding whitewater.

Catamaran Rafts. The idea of simply using a couple of inflatable tubes with a frame to hold them together—allowing the water to flow into the boat and drain back into the river—probably first began when Colorado River outfitters used the huge military-surplus pontoons (most over 30 feet long) to ply the waters of the Grand Canyon. A number of the rafting outfitters in California then started using shorter tubes in the 13- to 15-foot range for their smaller volume rivers.

The primary advantage of catamaran rafts is obvious: they eliminate the need for bailing. This, of course, makes them impossible to swamp because they cannot be filled with great volumes of water and rendered sluggish. The open center used on most of the newer models may seem awkward if you're used to a floor beneath your feet, and

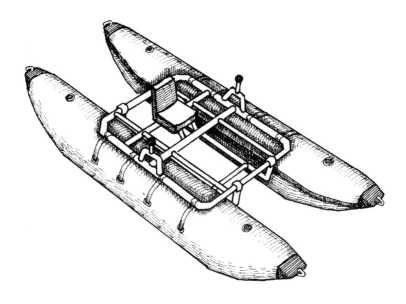

many boaters build a floor into the frame. A floor not only allows for better footing when boaters walk around in the raft, but also keeps them from getting as wet, and perhaps even from falling through the center of the boat and into the river.

Advocates of the catamaran also claim that the boat is ideal for rocky rivers with a steep gradient, where the chance of hitting rocks is reduced by 50 percent because the raft actually straddles them. And when a catamaran is pinned against a rock or canyon wall, its design permits water to pour through its open center, rather than filling the boat with water and wedging it even more tightly.

On the other hand, the catamaran cannot be loaded as heavily as a floored raft of the same size because it doesn't have the flotation provided by a floor resting on the water's surface. Many boaters also feel that catamaran rafts are more sluggish (the current doesn't have as much purchase on the tubes as a full-bodied raft), and even slightly more difficult to maneuver once the boat moves perpendicular to the main current, because the current exerts an exaggerated influence on the downstream tube as water pushes through the open floor and piles up against it.

Materials

Rafts are made of coated fabrics. The base fiber of the fabric provides the material's strength and resistance to tearing, while the coating provides airtightness and resistance to abrasion. Cotton canvas was the base fiber first used on military rafts, but it was soon replaced by nylon, which is still the most common, though polyester is used increasingly because of its stiffness.

For coatings, neoprene, a chloroprene polymer, was the standard for many years, and it is still available. However, it has been displaced to some extent by Hypalon, a more durable (and expensive) polyethylene polymer made by du Pont. More recently, even newer

A river raft is a simple, but sophisticated water craft.

"plastic" coatings have appeared. Polyvinyl chloride (PVC) and polyurethane are the most common.

The base fabric of inflatables is usually described either in terms of weight per square yard or in the more commonly used specification, *denier*, a unit of measurement for the thickness of the yarn. Though denier is used to describe size, it is expressed in terms of weight. Denier is the weight in grams of 9,000 meters of yard; the higher the denier number, the coarser the yarn. While it is commonly thought that the higher the denier number, the stronger the fabric, it should not be the sole consideration when assessing the durability of a raft. Other factors like type of fabric used and the reputation of the manufacturer should also be kept in mind.

The same precaution relating to denier also applies to fabric coatings. Neoprene, Hypalon, PVC, and polyurethane are all generic names which encompass a wide variety of polymers within each group. There are more than 20 neoprene polymers, 4 Hypalons, and several PVCs and polyurethanes available. Each of these basic polymers is compounded by adding different ingredients in various amounts to achieve certain characteristics. For example, many Hypalons actually contain a large percentage of neoprene. Therefore, it is impossible to generalize concerning the desirability of a coating without knowing the characteristics of the particular compound used.

An accurate comparison of finished materials requires examining standards of physical characteristics, like minimum tensile and tear strength, but these have not yet been established by the textile industry. Instead, we are forced to rely on the reputation and warranty of the manufacturer to produce rafts that will withstand the ravages of rocks and whitewater.

FRAMES

A raft is a spineless creature until you add its backbone—the frame. When it is equipped with a frame, the raft offers the advantages of both a flexible and a rigid craft. Its flexibility allows it to bend and fold as it encounters large rapids, boulders, and rocks, while the frame provides a more rigid and independent system of control which remains stable, despite the contortions of the raft.

All rowed rafts require frames. They provide the structure on which to attach the oarlocks.

Raft frames are also valuable on paddle rafts not only because they add structural rigidity but also because the frame enables gear to be secured above the raft's floor, preventing the possibility of a tear, and reducing distortions of the bottom of the boat that may interfere with maneuverability.

Most frames are made of either steel or aluminum, materials which are not only sturdy, but can be molded into a variety of shapes to suit the needs of the individual rafter. The frames' finish, too, is maintenance-free, which eliminates the constant coatings of varnish or

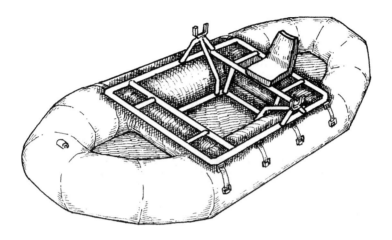

All rowed rafts require frames because it is the frame that provides the structure on which the oarlocks are attached. The frame also provides a raft with an independent system which remains stable, despite the contortions of the raft.

enamel needed to protect wooden frames from rotting. Steel frames are slightly heavier but less expensive than aluminum frames.

The designs of ready-made frames have progressed remarkably in recent years. Many models incorporate either an ice chest or aluminum dry box as a rowing seat, with another chest or box used as a front cross-tube, which allows for additional storage. Many boaters also appreciate the frame's arrangement for footholds when they are in heavy whitewater.

OARS

Oars are amazingly simple. Yet, when placed in the hands of a skilled rower, an oar becomes a thing of grace and beauty as it is used to finesse a boat through whitewater.

The grace of rowing with a pair of oars.

Oar performance is largely the result of its material. Wood is the traditional material, but aluminum and fiberglass oars are increasingly popular.

Wood

Wood oars—made of either a solid piece of wood or several strips of wood glued together and laminated—remain the standby, and many boaters wouldn't think of using anything else. The greatest advantages of wood oars are their good looks and an agreeable flexibility while rowing. A high-quality solid wood oar is also extremely strong, durable, and flexible, but it is heavy. Wood laminate oars are lighter in weight and still very durable, but are less flexible.

However, the quality of wood varies widely not only among different species of trees, but from tree to tree, and even log to log. Therefore it is possible to get a wooden oar with flaws in the grain. Wood also has a tendency to warp in storage, and the better hardwood oars, such as ash, that don't warp are quite expensive.

For heavy-duty use, solid ash oars or a laminated combination of ash and fir oars are considered the best choices. Ash is an extremely tough hardwood, while fir is very strong for a softwood. These sturdy oars are available in various diameters, which allows boaters to choose according to their use; thicker oars are stronger, but stiffer. A laminated finish needs to be maintained to protect the wood.

Aluminum

Aluminum isn't as aesthetically pleasing as wood, but it is a workhorse. Oars with heavy-gauge aluminum shafts and plastic blades have increased in popularity, probably because synthetics can be manufactured to more consistent standards than wood.

Many boaters consider aluminum shafts (usually plastic-coated to prevent oxidation) to be stronger than wood. It's not that a good-quality wood oar will break under heavy use, but it is generally thought that aluminum will absorb more of the impact of rowing. Aluminum also resists deterioration better than wood, and varnish or paint aren't needed to protect its finish.

Aluminum oars are lightweight as well, and a pair might easily weigh several pounds less than their wood equivalent. After rowing all day, the difference in weight is only too evident to the arms, shoulders, and back muscles. The plastic blades on aluminum oars are easily replaced in the event of damage, or even just for a change of blade width. Shaft extensions permit lengthening the oar for various river conditions and different boats, and the break-down models make for more compact transportation.

But aluminum oars aren't without their shortcomings either. Some rowers prefer the flex of wood and object to the stiffness of aluminum. Oar rigidity tires out rowing muscles. The aluminum oar is also difficult to repair in the field because it must be welded.

Fiberglass

Even newer than aluminum oar shafts are those made of fiberglass.

A fiberglass oar is unique because it can be manufactured to consistent standards (unlike a wood oar) but still feature a flexible "spring" similar to wood. Fiberglass oars are thus less tiring to use than oars made of aluminum or laminated wood. Repair on site is easy with fiberglass tape and resin. (Fiberglass tape and resin can also be used to repair wooden oars or paddles.)

Although fiberglass oars have yet to gain the popularity of wooden or aluminum oars, their advantages will inevitably attract more boaters in the future. Many boaters see fiberglass as the perfect compromise: it combines the flex of wood with the strength and low maintenance of aluminum.

OARLOCKS

Oarlocks do the obvious job of holding oars in place. As with other rafting gear, there are a number of choices available—and thus a lively controversy arises. Two contenders vie for the top spot: oarhorns and thole-pins with clips.

Oarhorns

The U-shaped oarhorn is the traditional—and still the most popular—oarlock. Its design is basic: the oarhorn simply cradles the oar as it moves back and forth in the water. Perhaps its greatest advantage is that it allows the rower to pull the oar out of the water and into the boat, especially when passing through narrow or rocky stretches of river. The oarhorn also allows the rower to make slight adjustments of the

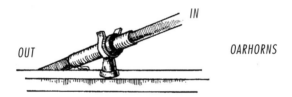

OUT   IN   OARHORNS

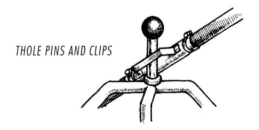

THOLE PINS AND CLIPS

OARLOCKS

Oarlocks hold the oars in place during rowing. The two types used by rafters are oarhorns (top) and thole pins with clips (bottom).

angle of the blade in the water, called *feathering,* that is sometimes helpful in reducing the friction of air or water on the backstroke (though large rafts are less responsive to this technique).

The main drawback of the oarhorn is that it requires your conscious effort to ensure that the blade stays at the proper angle in the water. Maneuvering the boat takes enough concentration as it is; you have little time to check on the position of the blade. This shifting blade movement can be annoying, especially to beginners; but a protective sleeve covering the oar at the oarlock—to prevent chafing of the oar—can reduce much of this free play.

Thole-Pins with Clips

Thole-pins, together with their clips, are the next most popular oarlock. They offer several advantages over oarhorns. The thole-pin is a metal rod attached perpendicularly to the boat's frame. A U-shaped metal clip which holds the oar attaches to the thole-pin. Both the clip and oar pivot around the pin.

Unlike the oarhorn, pins and clips are easy to use because the blade of the oar is held in a fixed position. And because the metal clip itself protects the oar, it isn't necessary to wrap the oar to prevent chafing. Usually, if the oar should hit a rock, a pin-and-clip arrangement will not cause the oar to break because the clip will pop off the pin instead.

However, even with these advantages, a lot of boaters don't like the fact that this system doesn't allow feathering of oar blades or the quick shipping of oars into the boat. As always, it's a trade-off.

PADDLES

Rafters use paddles like those used by canoeists. However, unlike a canoeist, the rafter who paddles sits, not in the boat, but on its tubes—either straddling the tube or sitting on it with both feet inside the boat. Like an oar,

Paddling a raft takes teamwork.

the way a paddle handles is largely the result of the materials used to make it.

Wood

Wood, naturally, is the oldest and most-time-proven material. As with wooden oars, boaters like the way it "gives" with the stroke—a feel they say cannot be duplicated in a synthetic paddle. Since wood does not assume the temperature of the water or air, it is more comfortable to hold. As with oars, laminated paddles made of strips of wood glued together are strong and lightweight, but lack the flexibility of solid wood. Its finish should be maintained at all times to prevent rot and delamination.

Fiberglass

The synthetic paddles usually have blades made of either a fiber-reinforced plastic or thermoplastic, which are both durable, lightweight, and require no maintenance. As for fiber-reinforced models, the fibers might be glass or du Pont Kevlar, or a combination of the two, while the plastics most commonly used are polyester and epoxy. Thermoplastic blades are usually ABS plastic or polypropylene.

Typically, shafts for these modern paddles are made of epoxy-fiberglass or aluminum. The epoxy-fiberglass materials, similar to those used in pole vaults, are not only strong and lightweight, but have a flexibility similar to wood. Aluminum shafts are durable and inexpensive, but also extremely stiff and therefore more tiring to use.

What size paddle do you need? Paddle length depends on such factors as the size of the raft's tubes, the height of the paddler, and the paddler's position in the raft (not to mention that intangible called personal preference). The most common lengths range from 4 ½ to 5 ½ feet.

Probably the most important aspect of determining the correct paddle is the paddler's height—the paddle should not be so short that the paddler must lean out of the raft to stroke, nor so long that the stroke is made with the arms above the head. Where the paddler sits in the raft also dictates paddle length. A paddler in the bow straddling the tubes has only a short distance to reach, while the one in the middle of the stern needs a longer paddle because of the long reach necessary to execute strokes used to steer the boat.

AIR PUMPS

Air miraculously transforms the limp and lifeless form of an uninflated mass into a sturdy craft. Getting the right air pressure is important because the boat's features are designed to work best and provide better maneuverability in whitewater at an optimum pressure.

Naturally, you must inflate a boat before its use, but you must stow a pump aboard the raft in case it is needed later. Since every inflatable loses a little air during the day, and because air contracts in the cool morning hours, the boat will normally require topping off before another day's run. And if the boat should be punctured suddenly, you will need an air pump to reinflate the compartment after repair.

Air pumps used for inflating boats differ from the typical tire pump because inflatable rafts require a large volume of air at low pressure as opposed to a small volume of air at high pressure for car or bicycle tires. Pumps vary from one another primarily in their method of inflation, ranging from sophisticated electric models to those operated either by hand or by foot.

Pumps also vary in capacity, and thus the length of time necessary to inflate a boat. Certain models can also deflate, which can ease the frustration of squeezing out that last bit of air.

Electric Pumps

When a power source is available, an electric pump provides the easiest method of inflation. Some models operate on standard household current, while others are clipped to a car's battery or plugged into its cigarette lighter.

A number of the best electric models are so powerful that they can inflate a 17-foot boat to a pressure of 3 pounds per square inch (psi) in less than five minutes.

Less expensive, less powerful electric models are available, but they often require topping off with a manual pump.

Cylinder Pumps

Another popular tool for inflating boats is the cylinder pump with a long hose, which works like a big bicycle pump. Most even have a foot-base for stability while pumping. The large-volume models are usually 2 feet high and 4 or 6 inches in diameter, while a smaller hand-held version (about 12 by 3 inches) is convenient for quick topping-off.

Cylinder pumps require some attention to ensure that they work properly. They must be lubricated regularly to provide a more effortless operation and to prevent the seal of the plunger from drying out and cracking. These seals are ordinarily made of leather or neoprene and should be lubricated with water, oil, graphite, or petroleum jelly, depending on the model.

Bellows Pumps

Bellows-type air pumps resemble a fireplace bellows, except that they have a long hose that connects to the boat's air valve. Operated by foot, they are easier to work than cylinder pumps, especially when pumping becomes strenuous as a result of increased air pressure. They are also more compact than the large-volume cylinder pumps.

RIGGING THE RAFT

Rigging the raft includes securing a frame, attaching oars (if you're rowing), tying down gear, and setting up bow and stern lines and grab lines. It's an idiosyncratic art. But the subject deserves some attention, because it is extremely important what you put where for reasons of convenience and safety.

Be sure to bring plenty of good-quality rope for bow- and stern-lines and for rescue lines. The amount of rope depends on the severity of the river; the more dangerous

Lashing down the gear is extremely important.

the river, the more rope you'll need. For an average trip, a 50-foot hank and a 100-foot hank are usually sufficient. The 50-foot is for the bow, for quick tie-ups; it eliminates handling excess rope. The 100-foot can be attached to the stern for remote tie-ups and a second tie-up at night. The longer length of the 100-foot rope is also useful for *lining* and boat rescue, both of which are explained in later chapters. On dangerous rivers where lining and rescue are likely, more is better. And every boat should have along at least one throw rope for the rescue of boaters.

The frame, whether used to support oars or stash gear, should be secured with nylon straps to D-rings along the sides of the raft.

Personal items needed during the day—cameras, sunglasses, suntan lotion, and a windbreaker—can be placed in smaller containers that are easily accessible. The first-aid kit and air pump should also be handy. And lunch.

Lashing down the load securely is extremely important. If tied down properly, gear should never be lost, even in a complete flip.

Pack the equipment so that it is as low in the boat as possible. Many boaters use floorboards of either wood or fabric. Some boaters throw a net over the bags to secure them, though it's a good idea to have a short line tied to each bag, just in case. None of the baggage should protrude from the sides of the boat, and the gear should not interfere with rowing or paddling. The load should also be balanced as evenly as possible on both sides.

Before you shove off, make certain the lines around the boat (called "grab lines") are in place. Be sure everything and everyone is on board. And if your boat doesn't have little holes in the bottom, indicating it's a self-bailer, don't forget the bail bucket and a spare.

CHAPTER 3

TECHNIQUE

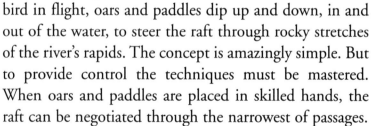

It's a beautiful sight. Like the wings of a bird in flight, oars and paddles dip up and down, in and out of the water, to steer the raft through rocky stretches of the river's rapids. The concept is amazingly simple. But to provide control the techniques must be mastered. When oars and paddles are placed in skilled hands, the raft can be negotiated through the narrowest of passages.

Finesse, rather than brute force, is the key to successful control of the raft in whitewater. Human strength is no contest for the enormous power of the river.

Eventually, with enough experience, the rafter strives for simplicity and grace, using the fewest possible strokes to guide the raft downstream gracefully.

OARS vs. PADDLES

There are two ways for rafters to move downstream: either with oars or with paddles, and sometimes a combination of the two. Oars permit an experienced guide to control the boat while novices go along as passengers. The guide (or experienced rower) sits in the middle of the boat and rows with the oars, which are attached to a frame placed across the top of the raft. The frame also provides a solid platform on which the rower sits.

Paddle rafting, on the other hand, allows greater hands-on participation as well as a good physical workout for all aboard. Everyone has a paddle in hand to control the raft. The paddlers straddle the tubes and make the appropriate strokes to turn and propel the raft downstream. Often there is a paddle captain who sits in the center of the stern's tube and shouts commands to the others, like, "Paddle right!" or "Back paddle left!"

Generally, a raft with oars responds more readily than a paddle-powered raft because oars can be backstroked more strongly than paddles can, largely as a result of leverage. But a team of experienced paddlers can negotiate almost any level of whitewater, and intermediate paddlers can easily tackle rivers of moderate difficulty. Paddle rafts, in fact, may even become a necessity on rivers that are too tight and rocky for oars.

THE FERRY

The term "ferry" means simply "to cross a river." In slow current, a boat may be ferried straight across the river; but in fast water, it is only possible to cross at an angle, rather like tacking in sailing.

To avoid rocks and other obstacles in the river, you must move the raft constantly from one side of the river to the other. Generally, rafters attempt to slow the raft's speed in the current because the slower speed allows more time to move across the river and avoid hazards.

To understand ferrying, think of the current as a straight line and the raft as moving directly down that line. The raft may swivel 90 degrees either way so that it is traveling in a direction perpendicular to the direction of the current.

The raft moves downstream fastest when it is traveling on the 90 degree plane (perpendicular to the current) because of the river's greater purchase on the surface of the raft.

Conversely, at a decreased angle of travel, on a plane more parallel to the current, the speed of the raft is slowed. As a result of the decreased angle, the progress of the raft across the river is also decreased. The best angle of crossing is typically about 45 degrees in relation to the

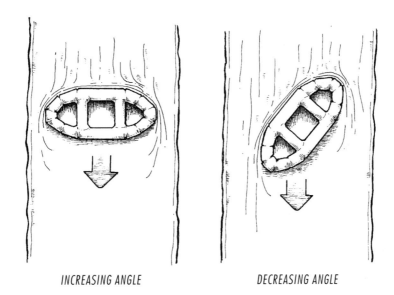

INCREASING ANGLE   DECREASING ANGLE

THE FERRY

To avoid rocks and other obstacles, it's necessary to *ferry* the raft from one side of the river to the other. The rafter usually tries to slow the boat's speed in the current, because it allows more time to move across the river and avoid hazards.

river's current because it allows both downstream movement and the ability to ferry.

The ferry position allows the rafter to avoid river hazards both by maneuvering the raft across the river and by slowing its speed. To circumvent a hazard, the bow of the raft should be pointed *toward* the obstacle to be avoided. Then the rafter rows or paddles against the current to slow the movement of the raft downstream. If a collision is anticipated, the ferry can be used to propel the raft across the river while it moves downstream, strategically missing the obstacle.

When running rapids, begin to ferry early enough to allow movement across the river in time to avoid obstacles. Minimize maneuvering as much as possible in large rapids. Keep the bow of the raft heading into large waves for the greatest stability—a raft that is even slightly sideways is susceptible to overturning.

ROWING TECHNIQUE

The traditional rowing stroke, the *pull stroke*, involves a pulling motion of the oars, with an oar handle in each hand. On calm water, the rower's back will be downstream requiring occasional glances over the shoulder to see what lies ahead. This position is fine for still water but is awkward in fast water, where it is necessary to keep an eye on obstacles downriver.

Early river runners followed the traditional method until 1893, when Nathaniel Galloway decided to turn his boat so that the stern faced downstream and row against the current to slow his speed toward oncoming obstacles.

Pulling on the oars while facing downstream offers several advantages. First, it slows the boat's speed downstream. Second, it allows increased visibility of the rapids and other obstructions ahead. And last, this stroke, known as the *pull stroke*, is a strong stroke, because it uses

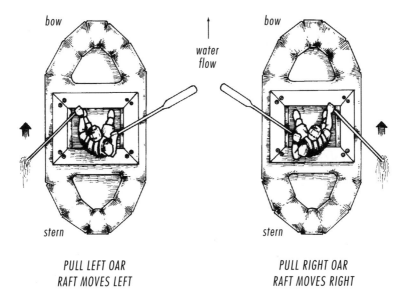

bow

water
flow

bow

stern

stern

PULL LEFT OAR
RAFT MOVES LEFT

PULL RIGHT OAR
RAFT MOVES RIGHT

PULL STROKES

The raft responds quickly to the single pull stroke on one side of the raft. Pull on the right oar, the bow of the raft will move to the right. Pull on the left oar, the bow will move left.

body weight and the muscles of the back and legs to power the stroke.

Basic Strokes

The basic rowing technique becomes instinctive after a little practice:

- Grab the handles of the oars and drop your wrists, causing the oars to lift from the water. Rock forward from the hips and simultaneously extend your arms. Keep your back fairly straight, head up, and eyes straight ahead. The blades of the oars should be no higher than necessary to clear the surface of the water.

• Straighten your wrists and relax the downward pressure of the hands on the handles to allow the blades to drop into the water.

• Now the power of the stroke begins as your body moves from the forward to the vertical position. At the same time, extra power is generated by driving with your legs. Your back and arms remain straight with your head level, as your trunk goes into the layback position. When your arms finish the pull, your elbows should be low as your hands come in toward the chest.

• At the end of the pull, a slight downward pressure on the handles will glide the blades from the water to finish the stroke. Then your trunk swings forward from your hips as your hands are thrust forward. Repeat the cycle.

Pulling on both oars at the same time will move the raft upstream in still water. In fast water it will slow the downstream speed of the raft. On slow stretches of the river, alternate stroking can be especially effective. The momentum of the raft is gained during the pull stroke,

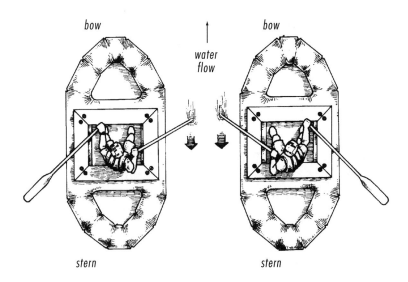

PUSH STROKES

A push stroke on one side of the raft is also effective. Push on the right oar, the bow of the raft will move left. Push on the left oar, the bow will move right.

but diminishes when the oars are out of the water. A more uniform rate of speed can be maintained by stroking each oar alternately.

The *push stroke* may also be useful in certain circumstances, such as in calm water just above rapids, when it may be necessary to accelerate downstream slightly without changing the bow-first position of the raft. To execute the push stroke, lean back, bring your hands in close to you at shoulder height, place the oar blades in the water, and push with a straightened arm. The push stroke is a weaker stroke than the pull stroke because it utilizes only the muscles of the arms and abdomen.

Pivot Strokes. The raft will respond quickly to the single pull stroke on one side of the raft. Pull on the right oar, and the bow of the raft will move to the right. Pull on the left oar, and the raft will move left.

A single push stroke is also effective as a pivot. Push on the right oar, and the bow of the raft will move left. Push on the left oar, and the bow will move right.

Double-Oar Turn

Pull on an oar, and the bow of the raft will move in that direction. Push on an oar, and the bow of the raft will move in the opposite direction. These basic pivot strokes are fine when used separately, but combining them gives added strength and speed. These combined strokes, known as the double-oar turn, move the raft easily, without any backward motion.

To move the bow of the raft to the right, pull on the right oar and push on the left. To move the bow to the left, pull on the left oar and push on the right.

It takes a little practice, but eventually this maneuver will become second nature. This stroke is especially helpful in turning the raft into the correct position quickly, before approaching rapids. It is also useful to keep the bow of the raft directed straight into the waves of rapids. This prevents the raft from moving sideways and possibly flipping.

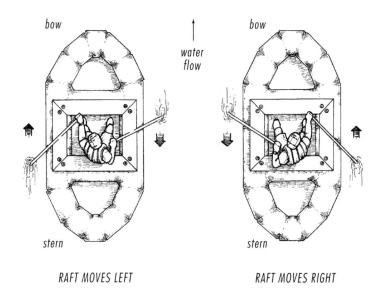

bow   water flow   bow

stern   stern

RAFT MOVES LEFT   *RAFT MOVES RIGHT*

DOUBLE OAR TURN

Combining the push and pull strokes—known as the double oar turn—gives added power and speed. To move the bow to the right, pull on the right oar and push on the left. To move the bow to the left, pull on the left oar and push on the right.

Rowing Ferry

The primary method of avoiding hazards in the river is to slow the raft's speed in the current and move across the river, thus averting a collision. Rowing ferry should be started early enough to allow the necessary movement for evading large rocks and reversals in the river.

If you wish to avoid an obstacle, point the bow of the raft toward that obstacle and row against the current to slow the speed of the raft downstream and move it across the river. Usually the best angle is about 45 degrees in relation to the current. A larger angle allows quicker movement across the river but also increases downstream speed of the raft. Decreasing the angle slows downstream speed but also slows the raft's progress across the river.

Back Pivot

The back pivot consists of turning the raft—usually with a single oar—from a ferry position to a stern-downstream position, thus allowing the raft to slip closely between rocks while moving backward. For a quicker response, use the double-oar turn.

Ordinarily, the raft floats downstream bow-first in either a right or left ferry position. Ideally, the river's width and circumstances of the moment provide sufficient conditions to ferry successfully from one side of the river to the other. In some instances, however, there is neither time nor space to change from one extreme ferry position to another. If the close proximity of rocks makes it difficult to maneuver the downstream oar, use the back pivot stroke. By pulling on the upstream oar, the raft will spin around into the correct position to avoid the obstacle. But because this stroke leaves the raft running backward, it should be used only when a forward position is impossible.

PADDLING TECHNIQUE

Paddling has become very popular in recent years, primarily because, unlike rowing with oars, it allows greater participation among a crew. Therein also lies its difficulty: you have several minds to coordinate rather than one, which requires cooperation among the various paddlers.

Forward Stroke

The forward stroke is the basic and most commonly used stroke in river running for both forward motion and turning the raft. The stroke is made close to the side of the raft, with the paddle shaft moving on a vertical or near-vertical plane.

Grasp the grip of the paddle with one hand. With the other hand, grasp the shaft several inches above the paddle blade. To begin the stroke, lean forward, extending your lower arm full length and bending your upper arm at the elbow. Insert the blade into the water as far forward as is comfortable. Place the blade fairly close to the raft and dip the blade almost completely into the water. Your lower arm pulls directly backward until your hand is near your hip, while your upper arm drives forward at eye level.

At the end of the stroke, your upper arm drops down, making the blade rise to the surface of the water.

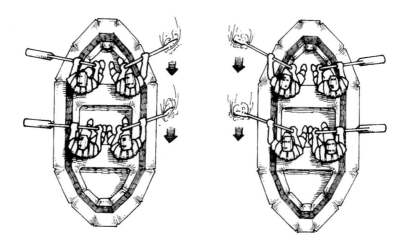

FORWARD STROKE

If the paddlers on the right side of the raft use the forward stroke, the bow of the raft moves left. If the left side uses the forward stroke, the bow of the raft moves right.

Then sweep the blade above the surface of the water to repeat the cycle. Your recovery back to the starting position should be made as close to the water and as quickly as possible.

Avoid needless body motion in executing the forward stroke; only a slight rotation of the body and shoulders should accompany your arm motion. Elimination of unnecessary body motion will allow greater smoothness and efficiency in the stroke.

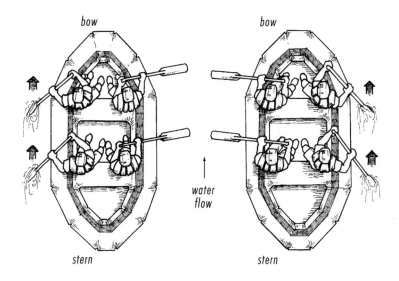

bow · bow

water flow

stern · stern

BACKSTROKE

If the paddlers on the right side of the raft use the backstroke, the bow of the raft moves right. If the left side uses the backstroke, the bow of the raft moves left.

Backstroke

The movements of the backstroke are basically the reverse of those used in the forward stroke. They begin where the forward stroke ends. Your bottom arm pushes down and forward while your upper arm pulls up and back. At the beginning of the stroke, your body leans slightly forward; at the end of the stroke, it should lean somewhat backward. The power behind this stroke comes from the muscles of your abdomen, arms, and shoulders, but it remains necessary to preserve a steady erect body position.

In still water, the backstroke will move the raft upstream. In fast water, it is especially effective because it will slow the downstream speed of the raft while allowing good visibility of the obstacles downriver.

Pivot Strokes

To turn the raft, you must learn the basic pivot strokes. If the paddlers on the right side of the raft use the forward stroke, while those on the left side keep their paddles out of the water, the bow of the raft moves left. If the left side uses the forward stroke, while the right-side paddlers keep their paddles out of the water, the bow of the raft moves right.

The backstroke is just the opposite: it moves the raft in the same direction as the side on which it is used. Therefore, the backstroke on the right side moves the bow of the raft to the right. A backstroke on the left side moves the bow of the raft left.

Double-Paddle Turn

Although either a single forward or back stroke will turn the raft, you can speed the turn by combining these two basic pivot strokes.

To quickly move the bow of the raft to the right, use a backstroke on the right side of the raft and a forward stroke on the left. To move the bow of the raft to the left,

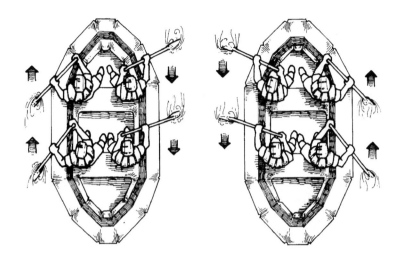

DOUBLE PADDLE TURN

The turn can be quickened by combining forward and back strokes. To move the bow to the right, use a backstroke on the right side and forward stroke on the left. To move the bow to the left, use a backstroke on the left side and a forward stroke on the right.

use a backstroke on the left side of the raft and a forward stroke on the right.

To negotiate these turns, your entire crew must be able to respond to the captain's commands of "Turn right" or "Turn left," with each paddler instinctively using the appropriate forward or back stroke.

Sideways Strokes

On tight, rocky rivers, you may have to move the raft sideways in addition to making the usual turning maneuvers.

In this case, use the *draw stroke*, which is a sideways pull of the paddle toward the raft. The draw stroke starts by placing the blade parallel to the raft as far as is comfortable, then drawing the paddle in toward you. It is especially important to grasp the shaft of the paddle firmly with your lower hand and to pull the blade steadily toward you. To move the raft sideways to the right, use a draw stroke on the right. To move the raft sideways to the left, use a draw stroke on the left.

The opposite of the draw stroke is the *pry stroke*, which is a sideways push of the paddle away from the raft. Start the pry stroke with the paddle blade near the side of the raft and with your upper arm over the water. Exert the push with your lower arm while pulling your upper arm in toward you.

Combining a draw stroke and a pry stroke allows the raft to be moved sideways quickly. These strokes are especially effective with smaller rafts in the 12- to 13-foot range.

The basic commands are simply "Draw right" (with left pry) and "Draw left" (with right pry).

Stern Maneuvers

A paddler at the stern can add greatly to the maneuverability of the raft. The most common function of this position is simply to act as a rudder—angle the paddle blade to the right side for a right turn and to the left side for a left turn. Other strokes at the stern, such as a forward stroke or draw stroke, will also make your raft turn faster. An abrupt forward stroke or pry stroke from one side of the raft's stern will make the raft move in the opposite direction.

Paddling Ferry

To avoid rocks and other obstacles in the river, you will have to ferry the raft constantly from one side of the river to the other. By paddling upstream using the backstroke, you can effectively slow the raft's speed in the current while watching the obstacles downstream. But the backstroke is a fairly weak stroke in fast water. To use the more powerful forward stroke, the bow of the raft and the paddlers must face upstream, requiring them to look over their shoulders to see the rapids ahead.

With the choice between a relatively weak stroke and poor visibility the best remedy is advance planning.

GROUP TRAVEL

Most rafters travel in groups of two rafts or more for safety. The raft with the most experienced rower or paddling crew leads the way, while another, called a sweep raft, with a competent crew aboard brings up the rear. Each raft should keep the one behind it in sight at all times.

While still keeping each other in sight, the rafts should greatly increase the distances between them while running rapids. Crowding together not only restricts maneuverability, but also increases the likelihood that one raft will collide into another and force it against an obstacle in the river. Keep sufficient distance between rafts so that if the first raft sees trouble ahead, it can stop before entering the rapids without being hit by the raft behind it.

This method of group travel works well for the rescue of passengers and rafts if an emergency should develop. After running the rapids, each raft can then stop on the shore and prepare itself for the rescue of the following raft should it be necessary.

LINING AND PORTAGING

If you decide not to run the whitewater, you must either carry the raft around the rapids—known as a *portage*—or guide the raft from the bank with ropes—known as *lining*.

Portaging involves a lot of work. It requires carrying the raft and all the gear around the rapid—often over rocky terrain. Lining is easier, but takes a little practice to control the raft from the shore with lines securely attached to the bow and stern of the raft.

Before lining, always lash down all gear securely. In rocky stretches of the river, lining becomes difficult because of tight maneuvering between rocks. In shallow areas, it is often essential to have someone push the raft along or farther into the current, while others maintain control with lines attached to the raft. In sections of the river with powerful currents and no obstructions, you can float the raft, with lines still attached but slackened, until it reaches the calm water below the rapids. Then pull the raft to shore, where the rafters jump in and continue downstream.

CHAPTER 4

ANATOMY OF A RIVER

The river has many moods: the *flatwater* stretches provide stillness and serenity, while *whitewater* offers challenge and excitement. Although the quiet stretches of a river are an important part of the experience, its rapids—of which there can be many—are more complex, requiring a thorough understanding of their forces to negotiate them.

Running rapids successfully requires an understanding of the river itself—its currents, form, and flow. Your knowledge of the river can then be applied to a knowledge of rowing or paddling techniques. This helps you steer the raft without mishap through the most challenging whitewater.

River hydraulics at their best.

RIVER HYDRAULICS

Rapids are created by a number of factors, including the physical characteristics of the riverbed and the volume of the river. The most obvious physical characteristic contributing to the development of rapids is the roughness of the riverbed, which is formed by rocks and boulders that have fallen from surrounding mountains or canyons or that have been swept into the main current by the flow of adjoining sidestreams.

Gradient

The gradient (or slope) of the riverbed determines how fast the river flows downstream. The faster the flow, the more difficult the rapids are to maneuver. The gradient is typically measured in terms of the average number of feet per mile the river drops from beginning to end. Generally, the greater the drop, the more dangerous the river.

As with any generalization, exceptions exist. Many rivers, most notably the Colorado River through the Grand Canyon, have mild gradients because of long stretches of calm water which drop suddenly into tremendous rapids. Other rivers feature high gradients, but the gradient is so uniform, or the riverbed so smooth, that the river is easy to navigate.

Gradient of the riverbed and its roughness are not the only factors that contribute to the formation of rapids.

Constriction of the river's current also plays an important part. This constriction can result from either the narrowing of the riverbanks or the presence of large boulders. Both confine the river to a more restricted course. Constriction of the river has the corresponding effect of increasing the velocity of the river flow.

River Volume

The volume of the river has a definite effect on the structure of the rapids. A large volume of water increases the speed of the river and the force of the rapids, reducing your time to maneuver and magnifying errors.

Generally, the greater the volume, the more difficult the rapids. However, at low water, a rock may be clearly seen and avoided; and at slightly higher water levels, it may be possible to float over the rock, which has created only a small wave. At even higher water levels, the rock may create a *reversal* (see pages 66–67) that must be avoided. At still higher water levels, the reversal created by the rock may be completely washed out.

River volume is usually measured in terms of cubic feet per second (cfs), which is simply the average amount of water passing a specified point per second. This measurement is relative: a smaller riverbed requires less volume to become suitable for rafting.

The volume of a free-flowing, or undammed, river fluctuates greatly in the course of a year. Peak flows of snow-fed rivers typically occur during spring runoff, gradually decreasing throughout the summer and early fall, but increasing somewhat with rainfalls. When running an unknown river, consult guidebooks or a sourcebook, such as *The Whitewater Sourcebook* by Richard Perry, to find the proper sources of information on the river's volume and its suitability for rafting.

WHITEWATER RATINGS

You will often hear rafters talk about the "class" of whitewater. Most rapids are rated according to an international scale ranging from Class I to Class VI. Remember, the ratings are

CLASS I:	Very easy; small riffles.
CLASS II:	Clear and wide passage; low and regular waves; good level for beginners.
CLASS III:	Clear but narrow passages; small falls; numerous waves large enough to cover the raft; some maneuvering required; suitable for intermediate rafters.

CLASS IV: Precise maneuvering required;
             difficult stretches of rapids; high,
             irregular waves; boulders directly in
             current; dangerous rocks and
             eddies; for advanced rafters only.

CLASS V: Exceedingly difficult rapids; long,
             rocky stretches of whitewater;
             completely irregular broken water;
             big drops; violent currents; and
             steep gradient; only for very
             advanced rafters, taking the greatest
             precautions.

CLASS VI: Experts only; not rafted
             commercially.

subjective, and may fluctuate wildly depending on drought or flood conditions and the seasonal water level.

These ratings, however, should be regarded for what they are: general guidelines which are subject to change. A number of factors can alter these ratings. Changing river levels due to snowmelt and rainfall, for example, can greatly affect them. Note the results of changes in river level on the ratings of several rapids in Hells Canyon of the Snake River:

Rapids	High-Water Level	Low-Water Level
Waterspout	IV	V
Wild Goose	III	III
Wildsheep	V	IV

In some cases, the rising water level increases the rating. In others, the rapids become easier to run in high water. On still others, the level of difficulty remains the same. Most rapids, however, are more difficult at higher water levels simply because the speed and force of the current are increased as the volume of water increases.

Cold water temperatures or extended trips into wilderness areas cause ratings to be understated. Beginners should note that these ratings are oriented toward boaters with previous river-running experience.

READING WHITEWATER

Rafters call it *reading* whitewater—the art of looking at, and then evaluating, a river teeming with rapids to determine which route through the boulders and rushing waters will inflict the least amount of damage to gear and to themselves.

Although the process of reading whitewater is an inexact science, at best, there are a few basic principles of reading whitewater which can be stated with some degree of accuracy.

Tongue of the Rapids

When a river tilts downstream and still water turns white, the current is usually the fastest and the deepest in the center. The friction occurring between the water and the sides and bottom of the riverbed slows the current in the shallow sections; while in the deeper sections, the current is swifter and more powerful because of the increased volume. This stronger current then moves rocks away from the main channel, creating the characteristic V-shaped lead-in at the head of most

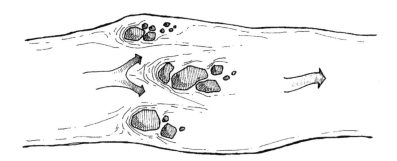

TONGUE OF THE RAPIDS

The *tongue* is usually used as a point of entry. The characteristic "v"-shaped lead-in at the head of most rapids usually points to the deepest and least obstructed channel.

rapids. This "V," called the tongue, usually points to the deepest and least obstructed channel and is used as a point of entry into the rapids.

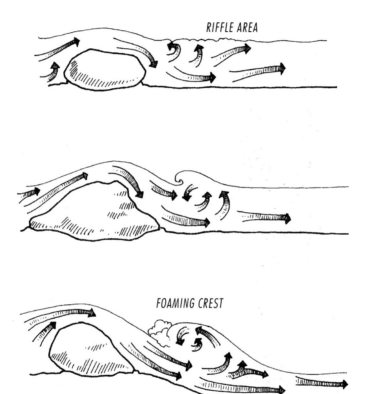

RIFFLE AREA

FOAMING CREST

REVERSAL

When water flows over the top of a rock and into the placid water beyond it, a back flow is created as it moves upstream and then back upon itself. This movement of the current on the downstream side of a rock is known as a *reversal*.

Reversals

Rocks that protrude above the surface of the river are easy to spot. But when water flows over the top of a rock and into the slack, or placid, water beyond it, the water creates a backflow as it moves upstream and then back upon itself. This movement of the river's current which appears on the downstream side of a rock is generally known as a reversal.

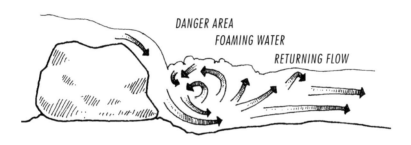

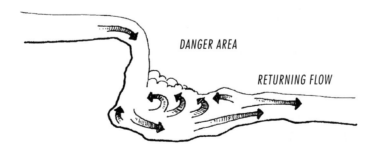

When a rock is just barely underwater, it may be difficult to spot from upstream because there is little turbulence created on the downstream side of the rock. Try to look for a calm spot in the midst of turbulence. Usually the rock will partially deflect the current; and, as a result, the water will level out as it sweeps over the rock. When viewing a reversal from shore, you will find that the downstream side of these rocks is often clearly visible. Other rocks, however, are concealed by spray and, with experience, can be seen from the river only by steady concentration.

If the rock is deeply submerged, a large reversal— commonly known as a *hole* because of its appearance —may develop. The deeper the hole, the farther upstream the rock lies. Large holes can flip a boat easily and should obviously be avoided.

Standing Waves

Water moves swiftly over steep sections and then slows down on more gradual inclines. When a fast section is followed by a slower one, the water piles up faster than it can be carried away. If the transition is gradual, this movement of the river creates turbulence in the form of standing waves. The size of standing waves naturally increases with the severity of the drop and the volume of water.

While standing waves are found throughout most rapids, only rarely are they high enough to cause concern.

If the wave is high but gradual, it is best to approach it bow first, allowing the boat to ride over the crest. If the waves are steep and angular, and might be capable of overturning the boat, it is a good idea to move to one of the wave's sides, which are usually more gradual than its center.

However, it is best to first make sure that the waves are, in fact, standing waves. Rocks just below the surface can create mounds of water which initially appear to be standing waves. Careful observation is required: standing waves have regular, predictable patterns, while waves which conceal submerged rocks are usually more chaotic.

Bends

Studying currents on a bend in the river is extremely important. Generally, the deepest and fastest current runs along the outside of the bend. This is why the flow of the water has a tendency to move the boat to the outside of the bend, where there are often large obstructions and other hazards, like downed trees, called *sweepers* and exposed rocks, called *strainers*.

Considering the force of the current, it is important to maintain the proper position and angle when entering a river's bend. Approaching the rapids from the inside of the bend allows the option of moving easily to the outside of the bend, where you can join the main flow of the current. Approaching from the outside, however, requires a difficult movement across the force of the current to the inside, if it becomes necessary to do so.

Eddies

An eddy is any current that runs contrary to the direction of the river's main flow. Eddies generally run upstream, behind either rocks in the river or projections along its banks. The slack water on the inside of a bend in the river is also called an eddy, even though the water does not move upstream. The imaginary separation between the main current and the eddy is known as the *eddy fence*, or *eddy line*. An eddy line can be very powerful and can even move the boat back upstream.

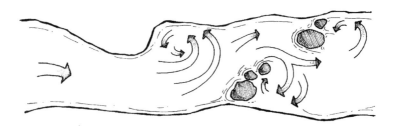

E D D Y

An eddy is any current that runs contrary to the direction of the river's main flow. Eddies generally run upstream, either behind rocks in the river or projections along its banks.

Eddies are useful when you are entering or leaving the shore, and they can be used to stop the boat while running rapids or establishing rescue stations. A few eddies are of the swirling, whirlpool variety and should be avoided because they are capable of trapping a boat and spinning it almost indefinitely.

PLANNING A COURSE

The obstacles and currents of many rapids can be seen clearly from upstream. Rapids which do not offer a complete view of their features should be scouted from shore.

Beach the raft well upstream and walk down to study the rapids ahead. As you reach a point parallel to the rapids, check carefully for rocks that will be hidden from view upstream, as well as the difficult-to-see rocks just below the surface of the water.

In viewing the rapids from either the river or shore, note the tongue of the rapids and the best point of entry. If entered correctly, many rapids require little or no maneuvering. While you are planning your point of entry, determine the direction of the main current in each section of the rapids. Note the hazards along the route.

Select the simplest and most direct route that follows the current and avoids obstacles. In deciding upon a particular course, consider the consequences of making a mistake. Choose the route offering the least possibility of serious mishap.

Once you have decided upon a course, note conspicuous hazards along the run for use as points of reference. Always plan an alternative course for each section of the rapids—just in case you make an error in maneuvering.

CHAPTER 5

SAFETY

Like many sports, rafting can be danger- ous. However, most river accidents could have been prevented if the river had been approached with a little foresight and a keen regard for established safety rules.

Very few accidents occur among the 3 million people who take commercial raft trips every year because the guides are professionals—after all, they do this for a living, and they know the river as their second home. Rafters on a private trip must know the proper techniques for the rescue of boaters and boats, should an emergency occur. Entire books have been devoted to the subject of rescue. Those who find themselves in the position of trip leader should read *River Rescue* (AMC Books, 1989), by Les Bechdel and Slim Ray, as well as *Class V Briefing* (Whitewater Voyages, 1987), by William McGinnis, two excellent books written by full-time professionals.

The most important aspect of safety on any trip goes beyond a list of do's and dont's. It involves an attitude that is established from the outset of a trip—that of a seriousness about safety. A more casual and cavalier attitude can lead easily to tragedy.

Leaders of trips have a number of special responsibilities all of which increase the group's safety consciousness. These include the collection of maps and detailed guidebooks, together with a good knowledge of the difficulty ratings of the rapids along the river. They must be aware of changes in river level and how these changes affect the difficulty of the run. They must obtain the approximate flow rate or river level. They then have to inform the other boaters of river conditions and determine if they are qualified for the trip. Last, it's necessary to review safety and rescue measures with crew members.

Leaders then have to plan so that all the necessary group equipment is included: life jackets, rescue rope, first-aid kit, spare oars and paddles, repair materials, and the appropriate survival equipment. They must file plans with the appropriate park authorities or make arrangements with a friend who will contact a rescue team after a predetermined amount of time has elapsed. Finally, leaders must also determine locations of possible assistance along the river in case of emergency.

PERSONAL PREPARATION

The best safety measures are preventive. And personal preparation is one of the most valuable safety measures. Good physical conditioning can help guard against everything from hypothermia to the fatigue which causes rafters to become careless.

Sharpening your wilderness skills, keeping equipment in good repair, and researching the territory you plan to cover—all are important. Still, accidents happen to even the most experienced rafter, and being prepared is just common sense. Wallace Stegner noted in *The Sound of Mountain Water* how a trivial mistake can lead to trouble:

> The rivers are not 'treacherous.' They are only forever dangerous. One who has not tried it finds it hard to believe the instant and terrible force that such a current exerts on a broadside boat out of control on a sandbar or rock.

Start on easy rivers early in the season and gain some experience before tackling rivers which require a great deal of maneuvering. And before running any unfamiliar river, research everything you can from guidebooks, maps, and magazine articles, to reports from the river's managing agency and other rafters you know. In this way, you can determine whether your level of skill is high enough to run the river successfully.

Once on the river, try to maintain a relaxed pace; a hurried trip is more conducive to accidents, especially when time is not allowed for adequately evaluating the rapids. You should know the proper procedures for rescuing boaters if they should get into trouble, and rafts if they should become lodged against a boulder. Be prepared for an accident which requires outside assistance by becoming familiar with the area before the trip and by carrying topographic maps in case you need to plot the best route out by land.

Finally, it is a surprising fact that the majority of river accidents don't happen on the river—they happen in camp. To avoid these accidents, use common sense and realize that the consequences of your actions are made more serious by your remoteness from the city.

EQUIPMENT PRECAUTIONS

Rafters who use professional outfitters need not worry about equipment, but individuals who decide to go it on their own must take several precautions. Of course, anyone who is not extremely competent should not go without the company of an experienced guide. Obviously, your raft should be in good working order before starting

Rigging a raft is an art.

off on a river trip. Make sure that your raft holds air, that your oars or paddles aren't cracked, and so on. All this is important, but especially so if you are traveling on a river you haven't run before. In the case of unfamiliar rivers, make sure that your raft, frame, oars, and paddles are rugged enough for the river you plan to run. One of the most common mistakes is tackling a big-volume river in a raft that is not large enough. The result is a raft overloaded with gear and people—a serious hazard.

Perhaps the most important piece of safety equipment is your life jacket. It should provide the greatest amount of flotation possible. For this reason, jackets designed for whitewater are best.

Rigging the raft is another factor in assuring a safe trip. Rigging is an idiosyncratic part of rafting, and there are probably as many ways to rig a raft as there are rafters. Although it depends upon personal preference as much as anything else, securing the frame and gear is necessary for both safety and convenience. Developing the best method is largely the result of experience.

In rigging the raft, any sharp projections that could cause injury should be eliminated. Sharp edges on the frame and rigid waterproof boxes should be padded with foam rubber. Also check to ensure that all ropes and lines are secure to avoid entanglement should the raft overturn. And obviously, provide well-placed grab lines for passengers to hold onto during rapids and in case of upset. Last, if your raft is not a catamaran or self-bailer, carry a good plastic bailing bucket and make sure it is securely fastened to the raft when not in use.

Rescue equipment is also essential in case a passenger is thrown overboard or if the boat becomes wrapped around a rock. Plenty of rope is the key to a successful rescue. For raft rescue, there should probably be at least 100 feet of rope available in addition to the ordinary 150 feet used for bow and stern lines. Mountaineering snap-links (called carabiners), which attach the rope to the D-rings on the raft, come in handy for raft rescue. For rescue of boaters, the new throw ropes are excellent because they float and are coated to provide a secure, nonslippery grip.

An adequate repair kit is commonly overlooked as a piece of safety equipment. This kit should include not only patching fabric and adhesive for rafts, but also materials for repairing other pieces of rafting equipment—frame, oars, paddles, air pump, and so forth.

SWIMMING RAPIDS

Even experts get spilled from their raft occasionally. So every paddler—especially beginners—should know how to swim safely through whitewater in the event the raft overturns. Here are the basic safety rules:

- If you get dumped out of your boat, hold onto your paddle and swim upstream of the over-turned boat. Otherwise, a raft full of water can pin you against an obstruction.

- Float on your back with your feet downstream on—or just below—the surface of the water. Your feet—not your face or chest—will meet any obstructions first.

- Stay with the boat—hanging onto grab lines, or whatever else is available—for as long as you need to get your strength and set your sights on a safe place to get out of the river.

- Let go of your boat and any other gear if it will drag you into a dangerous situation. Everything except you can be replaced.

- Swim to shore on your back using a backstroke, or headfirst, using a scissors-kick.

- If you're about to get swept into a sweeper or strainer, face forward and try to climb up onto it so you aren't swept underneath and trapped.

- If you are headed for a big drop, tuck yourself into a ball by clutching your knees and pulling your head to your knees. This will protect your body if you hit the river bottom as you are flushed out of the recirculating current.

- Don't try to stand until the water is less than knee deep. If your feet get caught under a ledge or between two rocks, the current can knock you over and hold your head under—even in a few feet of water.

HYPOTHERMIA

On a cold day on the river hypothermia is a real threat. How do you know if you are suffering from hypothermia? According to Dr. James A. Wilkerson, author of *Medicine for Mountaineering*:

Early signs may be undue fatigue, weakness, slowness of gait, apathy, forgetfulness, and confusion. These symptoms must not be negligently ascribed to fatigue or altitude. In hypothermia, shivering may not occur, especially during heavy physical activity.

In hypothermia, your body's temperature falls to a dangerous level. Any boater exposed to cold weather—and especially cold water—can become a victim.

Once your body falls into icy water, your brain automatically begins to conserve body heat by constricting blood vessels in the arms and legs. You begin to shiver as your body uses whatever energy is available to generate heat quickly. Then your body's core temperature begins to drop. As it falls below 95 degrees, there is difficulty with speech. Further decreases bring on muscle stiffness, irrational thinking, amnesia, and unconsciousness. A body temperature below 78 degrees means death. In near-freezing water, the time from immersion to death can be as short as ten minutes.

Dr. Wilkerson makes the case for being alert to the possibility of hypothermia: "Awareness of the causes of hypothermia and the rapidity with which fatal hypothermia can develop is the most important aspect of prevention."

If someone in your party becomes hypothermic, begin treatment immediately. First, get him or her out of the water immediately. Remove wet clothing and, if possible, replace it with dry. Move the victim into a warm shelter or tent and help get him or her warm. In more advanced stages of hypothermia (characterized by difficulty with speech), the person may not be able to generate his or her own body heat. Hot liquids may help, but *never offer alcoholic drinks!* They cause the blood vessels to dilate, allowing even greater heat loss. Build a fire. If that is impossible, body heat from another person, lightly clothed for best results, is crucial. If the person becomes unconscious, the situation is dire, and immediate hospitalization is necessary. Out on a remote river, getting to a hospital quickly, or even being able to call for help, might be difficult; so prevention may be a lifesaver.

Adequate clothing, proper food, and good physical conditioning can all help prevent hypothermia. The best clothing, because of their excellent insulation, is a neoprene wet suit or a dry suit (a nylon bodysuit with tight-fitting closures at the wrists, ankles, and neck). Consult the clothing section in this chapter for more details. The food you eat is also important: sugar and carbohydrates are metabolized by the body more quickly to provide heat and energy than are fats. So keep snack foods like energy bars handy to help stoke the fire, so to speak. Physical conditioning is also extremely valuable. A person who is not only physically stronger, but whose cardiovascular system is better able to withstand stress, will very likely be able to get out of the water more quickly and with less injury, or even pull someone else out of the water with less difficulty, than a person who is less fit. It pays to stay in shape.

LIFE JACKETS

Few items of boating gear have progressed more in comfort and safety than the life jacket.

Life jackets, or "personal flotation devices," have been classified by the U.S. Coast Guard. Type I is the old, bulky, orange "Mae West" jacket, usually filled with vinyl packets of kapok; Type II is the horse-collar version, which is unsuitable for river use; and Type IV is a buoyant

seat cushion, unsuitable for just about everything. The kayaking jackets, classified by the U.S. Coast Guard as Type III buoyant devices, are generally thinner and more comfortable to wear, but offer less flotation, than most jackets designed for rafting, which are placed in the Type V classification. Rafting jackets are specialized for whitewater use because of their additional flotation.

There are many features to keep in mind when selecting your life vest. Wear a model that fits as snugly as possible, yet is still comfortable. It will be less likely to get pulled off if you are caught in the recirculating waves of a big rapid. The amount of flotation your jacket provides also comes into play. The more flotation a jacket has, the faster it will bring you to the surface. The recently developed "high-flotation" jackets are a good idea on rivers with difficult whitewater. Brightly colored jackets are best because they are easier to spot in a rescue.

When wearing the jacket, keep all of its buckles and clips securely fastened. Pull all straps tight and tuck in any loose cords to avoid entangling yourself with the raft's frame, should you overturn.

CLOTHING

Veteran river runners generally agree when it comes to clothing: buy the best. A boater's enjoyment of the out-of-doors is too dependent on climate and water temperature to do otherwise. With new synthetic fabrics and insulation incorporated into clothing designed just for river runners, there is no reason to be uncomfortable.

In the tropics, you can wear just about anything safely. But less-pleasant conditions of cold water and air abound in temperate climes, even in the summer months. Wool works well for a natural fabric because of the empty space trapped in its fibers, which wicks moisture away from the skin.

The most versatile system is one that involves layering, allowing layers of clothing to be added or removed to accommodate changes in the body's own generated heat during alternating periods of rest and exertion. A jacket or sweater that zips or unbuttons also provides good thermostatic control.

The standard strategy for all but the warmest weather is to (1) start with an inner layer of long underwear; (2) add additional layers of insulation, as needed; and (3) top it off with a waterproof shell of some kind.

Synthetic fabrics have the advantage of being quick to dry because they don't retain water. Pile and fleece made of either polyester or nylon—under a number of trade names such as Synchilla and Polar Plus—work well as insulation.

The differences between these materials are negligible—at least to a layman's eyes. Their effectiveness is largely dependent on their thickness. These synthetics are extremely rugged and require little care. The only drawback of modern synthetics is their bulk: they don't compress well for packing.

Polypropylene underwear has become especially popular because it keeps moisture off the skin. Polyester fabrics, under trade names such as Capilene, have been offered as alternatives to polypropylene because they pill less and remain softer longer.

Although the thickness of polypropylene or polyester doesn't offer much insulation, your body is much warmer when it remains dry. Several manufacturers offer different weights of underwear for different climates.

In even colder weather, you can add additional layers of the thinner synthetic fabrics, or you can use a thicker synthetic insulation—such as Fiberfil or PolarGuard. Buying equipment made by a reputable, well-established manufacturer is the best assurance of quality.

For use on the river, goose or duck down is virtually useless because once it gets wet, it takes days to dry. Wool is still considered a good insulator when it is wet, though it becomes heavy and stretches. It is also slow to dry.

Regardless of the inner layers, a waterproof and windproof outer layer—in the form of raincoat and pants, paddling jacket, or dry suit—is needed to keep the inner layers dry and to prevent heat loss through evaporation. According to clothing experts, wool is hardly warmer than cotton unless you cover it with a waterproof shell of some kind. Kayakers long ago recognized the advantages of a coated-nylon shell when they developed the paddling jacket, with its tight-fitting closures at wrists and neck. There are now such a large number of paddling jackets and pants on the market—made with an infinite variety of fabrics and features—that the only problem is making a final choice.

The logical extension of the paddling jacket is a pair of paddling pants, complete with ankle cuffs of neoprene and a drawstring waist. Slightly more refined are pants with dry-suit seals at the ankles.

And don't forget the extremities—head, hands, feet. Any exposed part of the body can be a source of heat loss. As the temperature drops, don't just add layers, but cover more exposed areas, too. Your head is the most critical area of heat loss; half of the body's heat can be lost there. Any type of hat will help, but a close-fitting wool watch-cap, or synthetic ski or mountaineering cap, is best. Synthetic gloves made of either polypropylene or polyester work well to retain warmth even when wet. Neoprene gloves are even warmer, though they can be tiring because of the fabric's tendency to spring back to its original flat shape.

Either neoprene booties with hard soles or neoprene socks and running shoes are probably the best protection against cold water sloshing around the bottom of the boat. A thin polypropylene sock liner will also help keep your feet dry. Neoprene booties, in a wide array of styles, have become increasingly sophisticated with features such as zippers, lace-up tops, stiffer padded insoles, vulcanized reinforcements, and heavy-duty traction soles. But if you are ever forced to walk a long distance from the river for help, the neoprene sock and running-shoe combination is probably the most durable.

RESCUE OF RAFTERS

In most instances, a person who falls out of a raft is able to swim through the rapids and walk to shore or climb aboard the raft. In strong currents, however, it is often advisable to have safety lines ready downstream for the rescue of rafters who are unable to swim ashore.

A variety of lines made especially for rescue purposes is now available commercially. Most are about 60 feet long and are made of ⅜-inch braided polyethylene, which floats. A brightly colored line is best because it is more visible in the water. Some lines contain additional flotation devices that also add weight, making them easier to throw.

These lines usually come in nylon bags with one end of the line attached to the bottom of the bag. To throw, simply hold onto the end of the line and throw the entire bag, which feeds out the line like a spinning reel. If you miss your mark, you'll have to try again. Before your second throw, the rescue line should be re-coiled. One-half of the coil is held in each hand. The first coil should be thrown while the second coil is allowed to feed out freely (with the remaining end held securely in the hand). The coil should be thrown with an underhanded motion for best accuracy.

The placement of the line in the water is very important. The line should be thrown slightly downstream from the swimmer's position, since the swimmer is moving along with the current. After the swimmer grabs the rescue line, a tremendous pull will be exerted on the line. If on shore, the rescuer should belay the line around a tree or around his or her waist while sitting down for additional bracing. If throwing the rescue line from the boat, the tubes of the raft can be used to brace the rescuer. If the swimmer, failing to catch the line, continues downstream, it may be necessary to follow with a raft.

RESCUE OF RAFTS

Should the raft become lodged on a rock or gravel bar in a shallow river, it is usually easy to simply push the raft off the obstacle. But if the raft collides with a large obstacle that protrudes above the river's surface, it may be more dangerous.

If the raft is headed toward a large boulder, for example, it is usually best to strike the obstruction with the bow of the raft. That way, the current of the river, with the aid of a few rowing or paddling strokes, will invariably swing the raft off the rock.

A sideways collision with the rock is a bigger problem. If this situation—known as pinning a raft—seems unavoidable, a few precautions can be taken. Since the current rushing against a stationary raft has a tendency to pull the upstream tube down and eventually submerge it, those in the raft should jump to the downstream side of the raft, which lifts the upstream tube slightly out of the water, allowing the current to flow underneath.

If the unavoidable happens and the raft gets pinned against a rock, several methods should be attempted until one of them succeeds. If the raft is only partially pinned, have everyone shift their weight to the side of the raft most likely to spin off the rock. It may even be possible to push the raft away from the rock manually. If that fails, place an oar or paddle into the main flow of the river to act as a rudder that will catch the force of the current. If these methods fail, attach lines to the raft and have someone swim ashore to pull the raft from the bank.

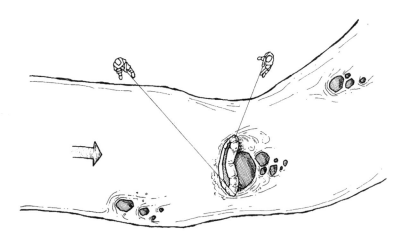

WRAPPING

The only means of rescuing a wrapped raft may be to attach several lines to the raft and then pull it free from shore.

If the raft's upstream tube is pulled underwater, it is more serious. This is called *wrapping* the raft. If the raft is only partially wrapped on a large rock, you may be able to stand on the rock and pull the raft up and out of the water. If this strategy isn't possible, or if it doesn't succeed, attach lines to several points on the raft's bow and stern, then swim to shore and pull with all your might.

If this still fails to unwrap the raft, deflate the section of the raft that is under the greatest stress and then pull on the inflated section. This deflation reduces much of the weight and pressure of water that is held inside the boat.

If all else fails, you may simply have to abandon the raft (secured to shore, of course) until lower water levels allow you to wade over and pull it free.

CHAPTER 6

PLANNING A TRIP

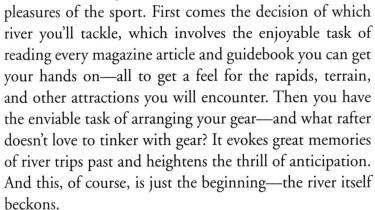

Planning a river trip is one of the great pleasures of the sport. First comes the decision of which river you'll tackle, which involves the enjoyable task of reading every magazine article and guidebook you can get your hands on—all to get a feel for the rapids, terrain, and other attractions you will encounter. Then you have the enviable task of arranging your gear—and what rafter doesn't love to tinker with gear? It evokes great memories of river trips past and heightens the thrill of anticipation. And this, of course, is just the beginning—the river itself beckons.

WITH AN OUTFITTER

If you choose to go with an outfitter, your job is easy. The outfitter will meet you at the river with all the rafts, paddles, life jackets, and other paraphernalia that are necessary for a trip down the river. Not to mention the food. Everything but your clothing and personal effects (camera, suntan lotion, etc.) will be provided. If it is an overnight trip, the outfitter may even provide your sleeping bag, sleeping pad, and tent, though sometimes for a small additional fee. And if the water is really cold, he or she may even be able to rent you a wet suit.

Regardless of where you go, you'll want to ask for a list of recommended gear. Here's a typical list provided by an outfitter for a five-day trip in summer:

1 bathing suit
2 pair shorts (fast drying)
1 pair long pants
4 shirts (long- and short-sleeve)
1 jacket or sweater
1 pair sandals (to wear in camp)
Neoprene or wool socks (worn inside tennis shoes)
Sunblock
Soap (carried in Ziploc bag) and shampoo
Toothpaste, toothbrush, and dental floss
Toilet paper (1 roll per person)
Hat

Towel
Fishing equipment
Camera and film
Ziploc bags (for wet items)
Moisturizing lotion
Flashlight (small)
Small pillow

Your outfitter will provide all the meals—sometimes you'll be asked to bring eating utensils and a water bottle—and the guides are usually quite skilled in outdoor cuisine. Most trips are actually on the water only four to six hours a day, so there will be plenty of time to engage in fishing, hiking, rockhounding, and other activities. Camp life is one of the more enjoyable experiences of multi-day trips.

Regardless of where you go or how long your trip, you'll find it worth the time to read up on the river and the surrounding area before you go. Grab every guidebook and history book you can find, and you'll be rewarded richly.

Selecting an Outfitter

How do you choose an outfitter for a raft trip? Keep two points in mind. First, look for a company that has been in business for a number of years, has a current operating license, and is an active member of a state or national professional rafting association. You will be safe in the hands of a qualified guide—very few accidents occur among the 3 million people a year who take trips with commercial outfitters.

Second, ask the following questions:

Costs. Make sure you understand exactly what is included in the price. Prices vary, depending upon destination, the trip's duration, and how difficult it is for the outfitter to shuttle you to and from the river. Expect to pay an advance deposit and the balance several weeks or months before your trip. Always check to see whether your deposit is refundable, should you need to cancel.

Equipment. Ask for a list of gear showing what will be provided and what you are expected to bring. Usually the outfitter provides all the boating equipment (boats, paddles, and life jackets), while you bring personal gear. Some equipment, such as a wet suit or wet-suit booties, can be rented from the outfitter. Meals are provided, and they are often superb, prepared by cooks trained in outdoor cuisine.

Seasonal Considerations. When is the peak time to take your specific trip? Ask about water conditions, of course, but also about foliage, wildlife, and river traffic.

Level of Difficulty. To assess the rigor of a trip, consider the river's technical difficulty and your expected level of physical activity. Longer trips or those which require you to help paddle the boat are more strenuous. You may even be asked to pitch in with portages and other chores, adding to the expeditionary spirit and physical challenge of the adventure.

A good way to initiate yourself to river running is to take a day trip on a mild river. Then, if the sport appeals to you, try more challenging whitewater.

Age Requirements. Most outfitters have minimum age requirements (usually somewhere between 10 and 18 years) for liability and safety reasons. Maximum age? As long as you are enthusiastic and your health is up to the challenge of the trip you choose, there is no limit.

Other Activities. A rafting trip is more than just adrenaline-pumping thrills. On most multi-day trips, you'll spend five or six hours a day on the river, so there's the rest of the day for games and exploration. Does your outfitter have plans to fill that extra time, or are you on your own?

Specialty Trips. Find an outfitter that suits your needs and interests. There are some that run trips that cater to large groups, some to families and fishing parties, and some that can accommodate those with a physical disability.

References. Finally, ask the outfitter for a list of references from satisfied customers whom you can contact.

Finding an Outfitter. For a list of rafting outfitters around the country, contact America Outdoors, P.O. Box 1348, Knoxville, TN 37901, (615) 524-4814.

By planning ahead you will ensure yourself a better trip. Start by deciding what you want. A white-knuckle ride? Quiet and solitude? Scenery? Do you want to be pampered, or do you want to be an active participant?

Then compare the way each outfitter responds to your enquiries. How they treat you as a prospective customer may very well indicate how they treat you on the river.

ON YOUR OWN

Go it alone only if you are an experienced rafter and plan to travel with at least one other experienced rafter. If you decide to go it on your own, the work increases substantially. But, of course, you will reap the obvious rewards of having accomplished it yourself. Here are a few last-minute rules and checklists to make sure everything goes as planned.

Personal Preparation

There is no substitute for this phase of your trip; you can never be overprepared.

River Knowledge. Have a realistic knowledge of your rafting ability, and *do not attempt rivers beyond this level.* Be aware of river hazards and make plans to avoid them. Your control of your raft must be good enough to stop or to reach shore before you enter dangerous rapids. Do not enter rapids unless you are sure you can negotiate them—or swim through them if you capsize.

Life Jackets. Wear a life jacket at all times.

Clothing. Dress appropriately for the weather and water temperature. Wear tennis shoes that will protect the feet if you are thrown in the river or forced to walk for help.

Emergencies. Familiarize yourself with escape from an overturned raft, swimming rapids, rescue techniques, and first aid.

Assemble a group. Never boat alone.

Leader Responsibilities

The leader of a trip has certain duties to the group—most of which, if followed closely, will allow the trip to progress downriver smoothly and safely.

River Conditions. Collect detailed maps and guidebooks of the river. Have a reasonable knowledge of the difficulty ratings of each section of the river. Be aware of changes in the river level and how they affect the difficulty of the run. Obtain the approximate flow rate or river level from the proper authorities.

Participants. Inform participants of expected river conditions and determine whether prospective boaters are qualified for the trip. Review safety and rescue measures before your trip.

Equipment. Plan so that all necessary group equipment is included. Life jackets, rescue rope, first-aid kit, spare oars and paddles, repair materials, and survival gear should all be carried.

Float Plan. File plans with the park service or with someone who will contact a rescue team after a specified time has elapsed without word from you.

Determine locations of possible assistance along the river in case of emergency.

Gear Checkup

The raft and its gear are your lifeline on the river, so it pays to give them your closest attention.

Equipment Inspection. Be sure equipment is in good repair before starting a trip. Test new and unfamiliar equipment before relying on it for difficult runs.

Oars and Paddles. Use strong, adequately sized oars or paddles for controlling the raft. Carry several spares.

Life Jackets. Use life jackets with enough flotation for the river you are rafting. Carry at least one extra per raft.

Raft Capacity. Respect the rules for raft capacity. *Do not overload.*

Equipment hazards. Eliminate sharp projections that could cause injury. Pad the frame as much as possible with foam rubber. Check to ensure that nothing will cause tangling if the raft overturns.

Lines. Be sure you have bow and stern lines, as well as lines for rescue and lining. Keep lines out of the way to avoid tangling.

Grab Lines. Provide grab lines for passengers to hold onto during the rapids and in case of upset.

Repair Materials. Carry sufficient repair materials for the raft and other rafting equipment.

Air Pump. Carry at least one air pump.

First-Aid Kit and Survival Equipment. Carry sufficient first-aid supplies and survival equipment according to the length and remoteness of the trip.

An Alfresco lunch on the river.

Checklists

Checklists are essential. Make lists of everything you'll need on a trip, organizing the equipment and gear according to categories: rafting equipment, kitchen box, personal gear, first-aid kit, survival kit, repair kit, and human-waste disposal equipment. The following lists are only suggestions—make your own to fit your specific needs and preferences.

RAFTING EQUIPMENT

Raft

Frame (and floorboards if used)

Oars (and spares)

Paddles (and spares)

Oarlocks (and stoppers if used)

Air pump

Waterproof containers

Life jackets

Rope (bow and stern lines, rescue lines, spare lines)

Nylon webbing straps (for frame tie-downs)

Bail bucket and spare (unless using a self-bailing raft)

Channel-lock pliers

Carabiners

KITCHEN BOX

Charcoal briquets (if used)

Dutch oven (if used)

Pots and pans

Eating utensils

Long spoon (for stirring)

Can opener

Drinking cups

Water containers

Fire pan with grill (if fire used)

Shovel (for dousing fire)

Camping stove and fuel (if used)

Knife

Matches (or other fire starter)

Plates

Biodegradable dish soap

Aluminum foil

Paper towels

Plastic bags with fasteners

Pot-gripper pliers

Pot scrubber

Water-purification disinfectants (chlorine or iodine) and filtering device

Newspaper and lighter fluid (if fire used)

Salt, pepper, other spices

Sugar and flour

PERSONAL GEAR

Clothes

Shirts	Gloves
Shorts	Insulated jacket
Long pants	Long underwear
Sweater	Wind/rain jacket & pants
Bandanna	Shoes
Underwear	Socks
Belt	Swimsuit
Hat	Dirty-clothes sack

Sleeping and shelter

Sleeping bag	Tent (with poles, stakes)
Bivouac cover	Tarpaulin

Other

Flashlight (with spare batteries, bulbs)	Biodegradable hand soap, shampoo
Sunglasses	Nylon line
Sunblock	Needles and thread
Mosquito repellent	Camera

PERSONAL GEAR (cont.)

Other (cont.)

Lip balm

Towel

Toothbrush, toothpaste

Toilet paper

Fishing gear

Binoculars

Knife (preferably multi-bladed and functioned)

River-style shampoo and rinse.

FIRST-AID KIT

Adhesive compresses (1", 2", 4")

Gauze pads (3" x 3", 4" x 4")

Gauze roller bandage (3" x 5 yds.)

Triangular bandages

Burn ointment/spray

Antiseptic

Aspirin

Eye-dressing kit

Tourniquet

Scissors

Tweezers

Cotton swabs

Snakebite kit

Adhesive tape

Band-Aids

Splints

Ammonia inhalants

Sunburn lotion

Ace bandage (2" x 5 yds.)

Butterfly closures

Razor blades

Safety pins

Moleskin

Salt tablets

Oil of cloves

Eye drops

Antiseptic towelettes

Calamine lotion

Antihistamine

Syrup of ipecac

Antacids

SURVIVAL KIT

8-foot tube shelter

Signal mirror

Whistle

Candle

2 firesticks

50 waterproof matches

20 feet of nylon cord

24 inches of wire

36 inches of tape

Razor blade

Emergency notes on first aid, fire building, shelter, weather and hypothermia

Waterproof zip poly bag

Safety pin

Aluminum foil

25-fluid-ounce waterproof container

5 dextrose cubes

2 energy bars

2 salt packets

3 bouillon cubes

3 herbal tea bags

3 packets of hot chocolate mix

REPAIR KIT

~~~~~~~~~~~

Patching material (1 square yard)

Adhesive (1 quart)

Solvent/thinner/cleaner (1 quart)

Small brush (for applying adhesive)

Scuffing tool/sandpaper

Rolling tool (for rolling down patches)

Scissors

Large needles (for sewing tears)

Nylon thread

Duct tape

Epoxy glue

Silicone rubber sealant/troweling compound

Bailing wire

Spare parts (vary according to type of raft and frame used, but includes such items as assorted nuts and bolts, valves, D-rings, and radiator hose clamps)

HUMAN-WASTE DISPOSAL EQUIPMENT

Surplus ammo boxes (rocket boxes)

Toilet seat

Heavy-duty plastic garbage bags (large and small)

Deodorant chemical (such as AquaChem, chlorine bleach)

Toilet paper, water dispenser, hand soap

CHAPTER 7

CLASSIC WHITEWATER

Not everyone understands our passion, of course. But for those of us who like their water white and foaming, the country is teeming with rivers. These are places to which you can drive, toss a boat into the water, and get wet!

While there are obvious whitewater meccas like Idaho and West Virginia, the geographical range for the sport is wide. And with a great deal of topographical diversity as well—extending from mountain valleys to desert canyons, to everything in between.

Here is a Social Register for rafters—a kind of Who's Who of rivers—offering a taste of the nation's most popular whitewater venues. I have chosen these rivers because of their status as "classic" rafting runs. Their waters have attracted boaters for decades. Their appeal lies not only in their spectacular whitewater, but also in scenic beauty, geological phenomena, and interesting human history along the way. Follow the current and dip your paddles deeply, for these are streams with lasting influence.

COLORADO RIVER · ARIZONA

River runners have long considered a two-week journey down the raging rapids of the Grand Canyon to be the pinnacle of river trips. Here, in the depths of the chasm, the Colorado River has been described immodestly as being the longest, wildest, grandest river trip in the world.

A float through the Grand Canyon is a geological odyssey of magnificent proportions; the farther you move downstream, the more formations of rock and time are exposed. The Colorado has been able to grind only a narrow, vertically walled gorge through the gradual uplifting of the strata.

In the beginning stretches, you approach several spectacular sights: Silver Grotto, a sheer chasm carved out of polished limestone; Vasey's Paradise, a fern-fringed waterfall that plummets from high above; and Redwall Cavern, a vast undercut chamber that is easily the size of a football field and which has been eroded from the rock by water striking against it for eons.

Then the world-class whitewater begins. The rapids of the Colorado have always been the benchmark by which boaters compare all others. The names of its rapids are legend: Hance, Hermit, Granite, Grapevine, and Crystal.

Then you encounter a scenic jewel called Elves' Chasm. Its pounding waterfalls, transparent pools, and lush profusion of mosses, ferns, and orchids are almost unfathomable in their beauty. Deer Creek Falls is marvelous. The waterfall here is spell-binding, dropping its wispy plume as it does 100 feet into a hollowed-out cave filled with ferns which vibrate from the spray.

Havasu Creek is one of the grandest features on this run. The dramatic impression you get from a glimpse of the stream below is the color of its calcium-rich water— a turquoise so bright it appears surrealistic.

Last, but certainly not least, comes Lava Falls—the rapid that boaters have had their minds on for the last 179 miles. The cataract itself is rimmed with a somber, glistening, black volcanic rock. Instinctively, your eyes move downstream—to the mass of jumbled crosscurrents, suction holes, and nasty, sharp waves churning below. Even the raw statistics are impressive: the falls drop four skyscraper stories, half of those in just 100 yards.

Your boat careers down the rapid and into the huge holes of the cataclysm, its boaters drenched by the wall of water that threatens to push them overboard.

Somehow you endure the intense pounding unscathed, and then camp below, with the churning flow of Lava Falls still in sight.

YOUGHIOGHENY RIVER • PENNSYLVANIA

On a thrilling day trip, the Youghiogheny's short, dramatic rapids have everything a river runner could hope for: steep ledges, big standing waves, and tight maneuvering slots through dense gardens of boulders. And yet these tough obstacles are interspersed with calm pools, where you can stop and collect your wits—along with paddle and boat, if necessary.

The "Yock," as it is called among its devotees, is a large-volume river with an amazing array of river hydraulics. It also has an extremely long season (at least eight months, and sometimes yearlong), so that when the spring runoff has diminished other rivers to a trickle, it still has Class III and higher whitewater. The scenery of pine and hemlock through which the river courses is also one of exquisite beauty.

The most intimidating rapids in the 7 miles of river from Ohiopyle to Stewarton are found in the Loop, where the river drops 100 feet in just one mile. Entrance Rapid, the Loop's first rapid, is a long, winding course of tricky currents where Sugarloaf Boulder, a huge rock, is set in midstream, ready to demolish anything that comes its way. Next comes Cucumber Drop, and then Railroad

Rapid, both of which are scouted routinely, even by experienced boaters.

At the end of the Loop, a two-mile semicircle that finishes just one-eighth of a mile from the beginning, or put-in (providing the perfect river shuttle), the boater can take a hidden trail to Fallingwater, the architectural marvel designed by the visionary Frank Lloyd Wright in 1933.

GAULEY RIVER • WEST VIRGINIA

The Gauley is born high in the mountains of West Virginia before it disappears ignominiously into Summersville Reservoir. Below the lake, the Gauley thunders out of the dam in a spectacular display of crashing water, which then proceeds to slice its way through a magnificent gorge of 1,000-foot-high sandstone cliffs, often called the "Grand Canyon of the East."

This is a two-day 28-mile run with over 100 rapids—50 of them are in the major league. The Gauley is a legend. In high water, its rapids are rated Class IV–V.

Five outstanding rapids punctuate the river. The first is called Insignificant, a misnomer if there ever was one. Pillow Rock follows quickly . This tough rapid drops 25 feet and is named for huge reacting waves caroming off the massive sandstone rock at the bottom. Nearby is the infamous "Room of Doom" eddy, welcoming paddlers who enter too far left.

Then comes Lost Paddle, a long rapid with four very distinct drops. Its undercut rocks are renowned for collecting stray paddles from upstream mishaps.

Iron Ring is next. Possibly the most dangerous rapid on the river, it was created in the early 1900s when loggers attempted to prevent logjams by blasting out the river bottom with dynamite. It received its name for a large metal mooring ring embedded in the rocks.

Finally, you reach Sweet's Falls. Named after Gauley legend John Sweet, one of the river's pioneers, this 10-foot waterfall must be run at a precise spot if you are to avoid being hammered by its gaping reversals.

Below Panther Creek, the Gauley continues 17 ½ miles to the town of Swiss at a slightly more moderate pace. However, there are still rapids to come, capable of raising one's adrenaline level, with colorful names like Backender, Koontz Flume, Upper and Lower Mash, Gateway to Heaven, and Pure Screaming Hell.

SNAKE RIVER • IDAHO AND OREGON

Between the Wallowa Mountains of Oregon and the Seven Devils of Idaho, the Snake River carves through Hells Canyon, the deepest gorge in North America. This magnificent canyon is bounded by beautiful cliffs rising from sandy-beach campsites framed by trees. Above the volcanic bluffs and grassy, pine-covered ridges are higher, sometimes snow-mantled, peaks.

The upper part of Hells Canyon is flooded by reservoirs impounded by three major dams: Brownlee, Oxbow, and Hells Canyon. Before 1967, when Hells Canyon Dam drowned the upper reaches of the gorge, the Snake was a strong contender for producing some of the toughest whitewater in the West. In a stretch of 19 miles, there were as many formidable rapids as any comparable distance in the Grand Canyon. Fortunately, persistent attempts by power companies to dam the rest of the river were rejected once and for all when Congress designated the lower stretch as a wild river protected under the Wild and Scenic Rivers Act in 1975.

The Snake River is usually clear and warm enough for delightful swimming. Often flowing at the rate of 30,000 or more cubic feet per second, Hells Canyon features several noteworthy rapids during a three-day trip. The first, Wildsheep Rapids, is found just 6 miles below Hells Canyon Dam, and it contains a hole that flips even professional boatmen regularly. The second rapid, Granite Creek, lies 2 miles below Wildsheep and is equally terrifying at certain water levels. The next 11 miles also contain a number of lively rapids, but the river slows considerably after that.

SALMON RIVER • IDAHO

The Salmon River pulses through the heart of the largest wilderness area in the contiguous United States. It is a cold and clear stream, flowing first through forested slopes, then through precipitous granite canyons pockmarked with caves.

Beginning as the Middle Fork, this Idaho river is fast, rock-strewn, and turbulent, and demands the utmost expertise in technical maneuvering and reading of whitewater. In June, after a winter of heavy snows, it becomes one of the most challenging whitewater runs in the country. Of the Middle Fork's 100 or so rapids, about 28 have names. Some of the more memorable include Velvet Falls, Power House, Pistol Creek, Tappan Falls, Haystack, Redside, and Hancock.

Congress recognized the irreplaceable value of the Middle Fork when it included it as one of the first ten in the Wild and Scenic Rivers Act in 1968. After completing a five-day journey on the Middle Fork, boaters can continue downriver for another five days on the Salmon's Main Fork.

Famous as the "River of No Return," the Main Salmon is one of the wildest and most beautiful rivers in the West. The canyon it carves is the second-deepest gorge in North America, deeper than Grand Canyon and surpassed only by Hells Canyon of the Snake River, also in Idaho.

Down through its mile-deep canyon, the Main Salmon idles, swirls, races, and thunders its way from springs and snowbanks in the Sawtooth Range to its meeting with the Snake in lower Hells Canyon. Along the way, the river claims the title of the longest undammed waterway in the lower 48 states.

The Salmon is a large, powerful river, dropping swiftly from the hamlet of North Fork to the town of Riggins. Over 40 rapids make the 80-mile run a lively one, and especially memorable are Pine Creek, Ruby, Salmon Falls, Gun Barrel, and, most notable of all, Big Mallard. Boaters can then float beyond Riggins into the Lower Gorge of the Salmon, whose 50 miles also offer exciting whitewater.

With these attributes in mind, most boaters have no trouble concluding that the Salmon is indeed a river to return to.

CHATTOOGA RIVER · SOUTH CAROLINA & GEORGIA

The Chattooga was made famous in the early 1970s by *Deliverance* and, living up to its reputation, it offers the best whitewater in the Deep South. As the river drops through a highland forest of hardwood, rhododendron, and laurel, it is also one of the region's most scenic.

Rising high on the crest of the Blue Ridge Mountains, the Chattooga plunges deep into mysterious and primitive landscapes. With rapids like the Narrows, Bull Sluice, Screaming Left Turn, Woodall Shoals, Seven-Foot Falls, Corkscrew, Jawbone, and Sock-em Dog, it is busy enough for the most experienced paddlers.

The river is divided into four day-long sections. The first section is usually too rocky for boating. Section two, from the Highway 28 bridge to Earl's Ford, offers mild whitewater, suitable for beginners.

Section three, which begins at Earl's Ford, is an intermediate paddler's dream of ledges, drops, and whirlpools 13 miles long, culminating in the impressive Bull Sluice Rapids. Section four offers dozens of blistering Class IV and Class V falls and is for experts only. This nine-mile run drops an average of 50 feet to the mile (200 feet to the mile near Five Falls) and rescue is extremely difficult.

GREEN RIVER • UTAH

Beginning high in the mountains of southwestern Wyoming, the Green River cuts quickly through Dinosaur National Monument before it starts its long passage down half the length of eastern Utah. The river lies in the vicinity of Canyonlands National Park, famous for sandstone spires, arches, and bridges magnificently sculptured by eons of wind and water.

The river first gained prominence when Major John Wesley Powell stroked wooden boats down its waters in his historic 1869 trip down the Colorado River and its tributary, the Green. Modern-day river runners can still follow Powell's trail; except for an irrigation pump or two, the river has changed very little.

On a five-day trip through Desolation and Gray canyons, the Green moves quickly past whitewater

Cleaning and airing out rafts at the take-out, Green River, Utah.

◀ Tatshenshini, Alaska

Usumacinta, Mexico

Loading rafts for another day's run, Rio Bio-Bio, Chile

Colorado River, Arizona

Nahanni, Northwest Territories, Canada

San Juan River, Utah

Green River, Utah

Salmon River, Middle Fork, Idaho

Rio Grande, Texas

Colorado River, Arizona

New River, West Virginia

Rio Bio-Bio, Chile

Chattooga River, South Carolina

Gauley River, West Virginia

Kennebec, Maine ▶

Tatshenshini, Alaska

Salmon River,
Main Branch,
Idaho

Cooking breakfast on the Green.

rapids of intermediate difficulty, with Steer Ridge and Three Fords the most notable. A number of ice-cold tributaries, lined with stately cottonwoods, enter the river, supplying clear water and good camp sites. You can see thousand-year-old pictographs from the Anasazi Indians along the banks.

Further downstream awaits a journey of several days through Labyrinth and Stillwater canyons, which cut through a massive wall of sandstone. Their steep walls are etched with smaller canyons begging to be hiked. The current slows here, as if to forestall its inevitable confluence with the Colorado River.

NEW RIVER · WEST VIRGINIA

The New River is not named aptly. In fact, many geologists believe that it is the oldest river in North America, and perhaps the second-oldest river in the world. (Only the Nile is older.) The New has also managed to slice through 4,000 feet of rock, making it the only river to bisect the Appalachian Mountains.

The New begins south of the Virginia–North Carolina border. As it enters central West Virginia, its character changes dramatically. Here the river pounds through the 1,000-foot-deep New River Gorge, filled with massive boulders and raft-eating rapids. The 15-mile day trip from Thurmond to Fayette Station is considered one of the wildest trips in the East, featuring some 20 rapids, many sporting eight-foot standing waves and vicious holes.

The first half of the gorge is mostly flatwater—with one exception—Surprise Rapids (Class III–IV)—which occurs about 4 miles into the trip. The rapid's double wave, which conceals a frightening reversal, is a real wake-up call. The action starts a few miles later, when boaters reach big Western-style whitewater.

This exciting seven-mile stretch begins with a couple of Class IV rapids called Upper Railroad and Lower Railroad. The next large rapids are the three Keeneys: Upper (III), Middle (IV), and Lower (IV), all of which have feisty holes to avoid. At high water levels, these three merge and become one long, terrifying rapid.

An infamous rapid known as Double Z (Class IV–V) soon follows. This is not only the most challenging, but the longest rapid on the river, with deep reversals and dangerous undercut rock. Then comes a favorite—Greyhound Bus Stopper. At higher levels this hole probably could stop a bus. Not far below is Undercut Rock (Class IV–V), with truly enormous waves.

The trip ends with an impressive view of the 876-foot-high New River Gorge Bridge, the highest and longest single-span arched bridge in the world.

TUOLUMNE RIVER · CALIFORNIA

One of the last stretches of wilderness whitewater left in the state of California is the Tuolumne, (called "the T") as it cuts through some of the world's most majestic canyons.

This swift and powerful stream pounds its way through a granite canyon that is three-quarters of a mile deep and filled with a seemingly endless array of gigantic boulders. The narrow, twisting channels end in holes that excite even the most jaded rafter. The scenery is truly spectacular: rugged gray walls headed straight toward the heavens and studded below with oak and pine. For diversion, there are the five-hundred-year-old petroglyphs from the Miwok Indians and deep pools loaded with rainbow trout.

The "T" arises in Yosemite National Park and races to the western Sierra Nevada to join the San Joaquin River. The most popular section is a day-long jaunt through the

18 miles from Lumsden Campground to Wards Ferry, considered to be one of the most exhilarating runs of continuous whitewater in the country. The trip ends, appropriately enough, with Clavey Falls, a Class V rapid.

ROGUE RIVER • OREGON

Rising in the Cascade Mountains of southwestern Oregon, the wild and scenic Rogue plummets through the rugged Coast Mountains, where it draws rafters from all parts of the country. The river's appeal is obvious at first glance: warm jade-green water, a variety of rapids, and dependable flows.

The abundant wildlife and intimate canyon walls make this a four-day wilderness voyage on which you are likely to see a bear eat berries off a bush, or an osprey dive-bomb the river and come bursting through the surface with a salmon in his beak.

The Rogue is one of the original eight rivers chosen to create the Wild and Scenic Rivers System. It earned its initial fame as a fishing stream. Its summer steelhead trout runs attracted anglers, especially fly fishermen, from all over the world—lured, in part, by the outdoor writings of Zane Grey, who lived in a cabin on Winkle Bar.

Then local outfitters, and an ever-increasing number of private boaters, began to discover the Rogue as a fine river to run for its own sake—for its rapids and campsites, its wildlife and side-canyon hikes, its history, and its dry weather.

Rainie Falls, one of only two fearsome obstructions on the most popular segment of river between Grave Creek and Foster Bar, is a waterfall that drops a full 10 feet in a single fall. But it can be avoided by running the man-made trough on the river's side.

The other rapid, Blossom Bar, is a gigantic rock garden immediately below the narrow, boiling Mule Creek Canyon. It looks terrifying, but at high water, you have room to maneuver. At low water, you will have plenty of time to make the right moves.

CHEAT RIVER • WEST VIRGINIA

The Cheat River, of northern West Virginia, has the largest undammed watershed east of the Mississippi. There are two classic sections for boaters: Cheat Narrows and Cheat Canyon. The Narrows is a five-mile section with rapids that range from Class II to IV, extending from three miles below Rowlesburg to Lick Run. This is a good stretch for boaters who are not yet prepared to run the Cheat Canyon, or when its water level is too high.

Calamity Rock, the first significant rapid of the Narrows, is also the most difficult. This Class III–IV drop has an automobile-sized boulder in midstream, which makes for difficult passage at any level. Below Calamity Rock are several rapids with five-foot standing waves at high water, and which require precise maneuvering at lower water levels.

Despite the attractions of the Narrows, most rafters come to challenge the remote 12-mile-long Cheat Canyon. This wonderful Class III–V run has a gradient of 25 feet per mile and offers more than 30 challenging rapids rated Class III or higher.

The first large rapid of the Canyon is Big Nasty, classified Class IV–V, and so named because of the huge hole at the bottom, sculpted by the 1985 flood. Then comes Even Nastier and 3 miles called the Doldrums. The river then pounds through Cue Ball, Zoo, Teardrop, and High Falls—another Class IV–V thriller. Then comes Maze Rapid and a flood-restructured rapid now called Recylotron.

The last major rapid is Lower Coliseum, where you can see Picture Rock, a huge boulder rolled downstream by the 1985 flood. Below the rapid, you will inevitably pause to admire the fluted columns of limestone—and to reflect on the wild day you have just survived.

SELWAY RIVER · IDAHO

The 49 miles of the Selway River from Whitecap Creek to just above Selway Falls traverses country as wild as any in the lower 48 states. With its pure, sparkling water and sandy white beaches, the Selway is a river of exquisite beauty. It abounds with elk, moose, bighorn sheep, mountain goats, and brown bears. The river lies along the retreat route taken by Chief Joseph and the Nez Percé

Indians in the 1850s, when they pitted their superior knowledge of the land against the firepower of General Oliver Otis Howard and the U.S. Army. (After months of fighting, Chief Joseph was finally forced to surrender.)

The Selway is one of the most technically difficult rivers in the United States. Laced with rocky, intricate rapids that require frequent scouting, the Selway demands supreme boat-maneuvering skill.

Difficult rapids are spaced throughout the entire trip. A particularly challenging series of almost continuous rapids are found below Moose Creek, where the river drops at a rate of 40 feet per mile. Wolf Creek Rapid is the most difficult rapid of the run, and requires a head-on confrontation with a serious hole that, in high water, has flipped even the big 27-foot pontoons used by commercial outfitters.

The Selway has a very short season—it is generally either too high (or snowed-in) until sometime in June, and then too low by mid-August.

The Forest Service has further restricted use of the Selway with a one-party-a-day rule in an effort to keep the river a true wilderness. During the prime season of June and July, as many as 70 groups apply for a single starting place.

ARKANSAS RIVER • COLORADO

The Arkansas starts out a tumbling and wild-spirited river as it flows unencumbered from the snow-crusted peaks of the Sawatch Range along the Continental Divide. By the time the river enters Arkansas it is a slow-paced, elderly gentleman of the Ozarks. But its Colorado segment is another story.

The river's source in Colorado's Rocky Mountains is a small stream which picks up melting snow from a series of towering mountain peaks, not far from the celebrity-studded ski slopes of Vail. When the rock-laden river reaches the old mining town of Leadville, it surges enough to accommodate boats; and on any day during its short runoff, the river is full of rafts and kayaks.

To the right loom 14,000-foot peaks in the Collegiate Range—Mount Yale, Mount Harvard, and Mount Princeton—and the river rushes through Pine Creek Rapids (Class V), and then a Class IV stretch, which is often the site of national kayaking championships. Next comes 10-mile-long Brown's Canyon, with its raft-eating Siedel's Suck Hole. Farther downstream, the walls open; and although the rapids diminish, the river remains a millrace, with few eddies providing escape. Finally, Royal Gorge encloses the river, with steep pool-and-drop rapids in quick succession.

An interstate highway follows the river most of its way, making access to it easy, but also preventing it from being a remote wilderness experience. However, for those with limited time who desire a day of challenging white-water the Arkansas serves well.

The easy access also gives a river runner contact with other boaters. While chatting about the day's run—preferably over a cold beer in one of the nearby saloons—one immediately senses a camaraderie within the river's fraternity.

NOATAK RIVER • ALASKA

If you are looking to get away from it all, many experienced boaters consider the Noatak to be the finest river in the Far North. And not without reason—its flow is entirely above the Arctic Circle.

The sense of isolation here is unparalleled anywhere in North America, as you meander across its pristine wilderness. The river is surrounded by tundra, narrow valleys, high mountains, and lowlands of birch and spruce. Caribou, wolves, and mountain goats roam the hills—and the fishing for grayling and char is excellent. The long days of summer eventually give rise to spectacular views of the aurora borealis.

Rafters slide their boats into these swift and relatively calm waters at the enchanting headwaters among the Brooks Range in Gates of the Arctic National Park. The river then flows over 200 miles through Noatak National Preserve, where there is not a single sign of civilization. The two-week trip ends at the village of Noatak on the Chukcki Sea, and everyone agrees that time has passed too quickly.

OWYHEE RIVER • OREGON

The Owyhee River chisels a patient path through the high desert of southeast Oregon. This is sagebrush country, a marvelous place of old lava falls and craters carved from layers of multicolored basalt.

The four- or five-day journey through these desolate canyons is extremely picturesque. Along the way are badlands, steep rock walls, and sandy beaches. In one 10-mile-long gorge, the cliffs soar 1,000 feet straight up. The only evidence of human life is a stone cabin that served as a hideout for cattle rustlers and a few dilapidated wooden waterwheels once used for irrigation.

There is a great variety of bird life here, with over sixty species identified, including golden eagles, Canada geese, and falcons. Antelope, bighorn sheep, deer, bobcats, and coyotes are seen frequently.

The lower stretch of river, the 60 miles from the cowboy town of Rome to the Owyhee Reservoir at Leslie Gulch, is the most popular. It is largely Class II and III water, eminently suitable for beginning boaters. You'll have lots of time out for side hikes and swimming.

AND MORE . . .

And there is more, much more. Here's a taste of other popular rafting rivers whose frothy waters beckon as strongly as any.

Kobuk • ALASKA

The Kobuk is said to be the first river in the Brooks Range traveled by explorers. With the exception of a few rapids in its beginning stretches, this is a leisurely float through vast wilderness. You will encounter moose, caribou, bear, and wolf along the way.

Salt • ARIZONA

The Salt offers some of the best whitewater in the desert Southwest. It is also an oasis in the vast Sonoran Desert for migratory birds, not to mention bald eagles, beavers, otters, and deer. It makes a perfect off-season river trip, as it is usually traversed in March and April.

American, North Fork • CALIFORNIA

The North Fork of the American is not only one of the loveliest rivers of the Sierras, but also one of California's finest and most technically challenging whitewater streams. The 14-mile-long Giant Gap run is one Class V rapid after another through a 2,000-foot-deep ravine.

American, South Fork • CALIFORNIA

From Chili Bar to Folsom Lake, this 21-mile, one- or two-day hop through Northern California gold country is the most popular rafting run in the state. Reliable flows all summer long.

Cache la Poudre • COLORADO

The Cache la Poudre tumbles from the snowcapped peaks of Rocky Mountain National Park as an exceptionally beautiful tributary of the North Platte. Magnificent towering spires and sheer cliffs adorn its canyons. The whitewater is continuous, with numerous technical rapids, powerful hydraulics, and steep drops.

Yampa • COLORADO

With its headwaters high in the Rocky Mountains, the Yampa pushes westward to Dinosaur National Monument on the Colorado-Utah line, where it joins the Green River. The last 55 miles are superb, carving their way through sheer sandstone walls 2,500 feet high and a number of rapids. Its most notable is Warm Springs Rapids, Class III–IV, which has been known to flip 33-foot pontoons.

Kennebec • MAINE

An intense, day-long, bob-and-weave through a 13-mile route that includes Class IV Kennebec Gorge. The forested scenery and virgin wilderness along the banks is magnificent, as is the side hike to 90-foot-high Moxie Falls.

Flathead • MONTANA

The Flathead offers a triple bounty for boaters: a North Fork, a Middle Fork, and a South Fork. Their currents form several boundaries of Glacier National Park, and all are exceptional for unspoilt forests and mountains. Its roster of wildlife includes grizzly bears, elk, deer, moose, mountain goats, and birds of prey.

Rio Grande • NEW MEXICO

Near the quaint northern New Mexico town of Taos, the 17-mile journey through the 800-foot-deep Taos Box Canyon is spectacular. It has many splendid Class III–IV rapids with names to match: Ski Jump, Powerline, and Rock Garden.

Illinois • OREGON

The Illinois is a little-known tributary of the Rogue. Its remote canyons are not far from the Pacific Ocean and the California state line. The river offers a complete wilderness experience of coniferous forests and lush ferns, with excellent Class IV to V whitewater during the four-day, 40-mile journey.

Ocoee • TENNESSEE

The Ocoee is one of the most popular day trips in the

Southeast, and for good reason. With 4 ½ miles of white-water dropping 60 feet to the mile, this river makes for almost nonstop Class III–IV whitewater action.

Methow • WASHINGTON

This North Cascades stream winds 16 thrilling miles through apple groves and canyons on its way to the Columbia River. It has quickly become one of the state's most favored runs, due to big standing waves, warm climate, and reliable flows through August.

Skagit • WASHINGTON

Located in the rugged forest of the central Cascades, the Skagit is a bumptious mountain stream. Its blue green waters rush through glacier-scoured terrain of open valleys and twisting canyons. Most of its rapids are crisp vertical drops followed by long chutes, which are perfect for intermediate boaters.

And in Canada: *Ottawa River* • ONTARIO

The Ottawa is the workhorse of the big, eastern Ontario whitewater rivers, delivering more than 60,000 rafters a year down its 5-mile, Class III–IV Roche-Fendu section.

FOR FURTHER INFORMATION

The most complete collection of information about rafting rivers—where to go, suitable flows, preferred seasons, guidebooks, outfitters, and so forth—is *The Whitewater Sourcebook,* by Richard Perry (Menasha Ridge Press, 1993).

CHAPTER 8

PROTECTING OUR RIVERS

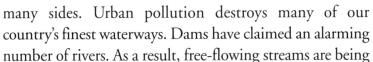

Our rivers are in peril. The attacks come from many sides. Urban pollution destroys many of our country's finest waterways. Dams have claimed an alarming number of rivers. As a result, free-flowing streams are being eradicated from the face of the earth forever.

But even the few rivers which have been graciously spared and protected by law are endangered by unlikely culprits—river runners, who have been accused of loving them to death. Overuse of what is surely nature's greatest resource makes it imperative that we take action to help preserve what little we have left.

Stress check: Vacationing on Earth's finest resource.

TRACELESS CAMPING

A study compiled by the National Park Service calculated the impact created by river runners in the Grand Canyon. Their findings are disturbing. The report notes:

> Human debris (food particles, plastic, etc.) is being incorporated into the riverbanks at rates that exceed the purging capacities of natural processes.

This causes beaches to look and smell like sandboxes found in heavily used public parks.

The study reported that campsites are drastically overused. Fewer than 100 campsites receive more than 75 percent of all use (among the more than 15,000 people who float the river each year). At some campsites, 30 or 40 people camp every night during the busiest four months of the year.

The Park Service also found that live, standing trees were being used for firewood. Ash and charcoal of campfires have been spread into the ground at rates that far surpass nature's ability to cleanse the soil. And over 20 tons of human waste were produced each year by people traveling through the canyon. Now such waste must be carried out of the canyon, but under previous park policy, some 5,000 human-waste burial sites were dug along the river.

Garbage. The rule for disposal of garbage is simple: carry it *all* out whether it's yours or someone else's. Keep a small bag handy for trash during the day, and be careful to collect even the smallest debris.

If you use a campfire or charcoal briquets, burn all trash possible. (Remember that aluminum-foil packets will not burn and that certain foods, such as eggshells, require more time to burn than a short morning fire provides.) If the garbage cannot be burned, dispose of it by placing everything except liquids in the garbage bag. Oils and grease should always be carried out.

Liquid garbage—coffee, soup, dishwater—should be strained first. The remaining solids can then be thrown into the garbage bag. In wooded areas, the liquid residue should be poured on the ground (at least 100 feet from any area normally used for camping). In the desert, where decomposition is slower, the liquid should be poured into the main current of the river.

Human-Waste Disposal. Solid waste presents an environmental impact and a hazard to human health. Many river-management agencies require all solid waste to be carried out of the river corridor. It is inevitable that the policy will soon be implemented on most government lands, and it's a good idea in all heavily traveled areas.

The system, which campers and rafters must bring with them, is easy to set up. A metal box serves as the toilet container, and the toilet seat is placed on top. A small quantity of a chemical deodorant is then poured into the box; it is important because it reduces bacterial growth and the production of methane gas.

Side hikes also require sanitary disposal, but of a slightly different kind. To reduce impact, bury the waste (after burning the toilet paper carefully) in a hole about 6 inches deep, which is the best depth for the soil elements that cause rapid decomposition. Carry a small backpacker's trowel for this purpose, and make the hole at least 100 feet from the river's high-water line and away from any area normally used for camping.

WILD AND SCENIC

The Environmental Protection Agency once tried to tally the total number of dams on America's rivers; it lost count somewhere around 60,000. That includes 15,000 private hydropower plants, 750 dams operated by the Army Corps of Engineers and Bureau of Reclamation, more than 1,700 dams on U.S. Bureau of Land Management lands, 300 dams on Native American lands, 170 in National Wildlife Refuges, and 260 in the National Park System. After adding almost 50,000 general-purpose dams, it's easy to see why the EPA lost count.

During 350 years of heavy European settlement in America, dams have become integral to our way of life. They create power, shunt water to our fields, and save communities from the ravages of flood and drought. But in our rush to reap the benefits of impoundment, some 600,000 miles of river have been drowned behind concrete and steel. Throughout the country, the wild character of rivers and their role in the survival of aquatic and terrestrial life have been sacrificed in the name of progress.

There is, of course, a long-established patchwork of national parks, forests, refuges, and wilderness areas to protect natural beauty. But in spite of these attempts at preservation, our rivers face extinction. It was in 1968 that Americans became concerned enough with the fate of our rivers to enact a law to protect them.

In 1968 Lyndon Johnson was president, the war in Vietnam raged on, and Dr. Benjamin Spock was indicted for urging young men to evade the draft. *Survey 7* landed on the moon. Arthur Ashe won the U.S. Open. And the Wild and Scenic Rivers Act became law.

America had definitely entered an era of environmental awareness. The populist phase began in 1966 with publication of Rachel Carson's *Silent Spring*, which examined the widespread use of chemical insecticides and pesticides. Tougher pollution laws, ensuring clean air and pure water, were soon enacted. The Wilderness Preservation Act was in place, and the National Scenic Trails Act was being discussed before Congress. The country was ready for a law to protect its rivers.

The concept of a system to save rivers arose during the early 1960s, when several congressional committees endorsed the idea. What was needed, said members of Congress, was a law to counterbalance the national agenda encouraging dam construction. All that remained were the details of the act; but that process, as usual, took several years. The act finally molded a long-neglected policy that certain rivers possessing outstanding attributes—of scenery, recreation, geology, fish, wildlife, history, and culture—be preserved . . . free-flowing for all time.

There is nothing complex about the act. It seeks to protect rivers by classifying them as wild, scenic, or recreational. It is a form of zoning; but instead of resolving disputes about urban sprawl, it focuses on sustaining the wildness of the backcountry.

But however important, the classifications are secondary to the real purpose of the bill: to stop dams. The teeth of the act comes with the ban on all federally funded, assisted, or licensed water projects, which includes dams, since they all require federal approval. But the act goes further, by allowing managers to control development of the river corridor in two ways: either through outright purchase or through scenic easements.

The Main Salmon River was included in the Wild and Scenic Rivers System since 1980.

The National Wild and Scenic Rivers Act was enacted to highlight—at least symbolically—the importance of rivers over dams. How well has it worked? Today there are over 10,000 miles of rivers throughout the United States that are protected from unchecked development by the National Wild and Scenic Rivers System. It sounds impressive, but it is less than 0.5 percent of America's 3.5 million miles of rivers. In fact, for each mile of river preserved, 85 miles have been lost to dams. Though in that light, the number of miles protected may seem insignificant, consider the alternative were the act not in place.

Initially, sections of eight rivers were specifically protected by the act: the Rogue, the Middle Fork of the Salmon, the Clearwater in Idaho, the Rio Grande, the Wolf in Wisconsin, the St. Croix bordering Minnesota and Wisconsin, the Eleven Point in Missouri, and California's Feather. During the next ten years, only eight more rivers were included.

A 1978 report of the Comptroller General concluded that progress had been "excessively slow and costly." Two reasons were given: federal agencies were taking too much time (an average of 6 ½ years) to assess a river's eligibility, and states were not acting on their own because of the high costs of private land speculation. (During a four-year delay on Washington's Skagit River the cost increased from $520 to $2,670 an acre.)

In addition to those handicaps, other problems exist. The act is powerless to prevent construction of dams upstream unless they "unreasonably diminish" the values of the river. This clause, of course, is subject to interpretation. A dam upstream may reduce flows to such a level that the resulting trickle can hardly be called a river. An example is the Little Miami River in Ohio, where dams on the unprotected Ash Fork and Caesar Creek tributaries alter the flow by 30 percent.

It is a misconception that the act prohibits dams in wilderness areas. In fact the federal agency managing the river, whether the National Park Service, the U.S. Forest Service, or the Bureau of Land Management, can overrule the wilderness designation and allow a dam. A case in point is Glen Canyon Dam on the Colorado, which flooded Rainbow Bridge National Monument. A dam in the Grand Canyon—though a national park, not part of the Wild and Scenic Rivers System—still looms as a possibility.

The act, unfortunately, came too late for a number of outstanding rivers. The 68,000 dams in the United States have already drowned some 600,000 miles of rivers that once were free-flowing and are now stagnant pools. By contrast, the Wild and Scenic Rivers Act contains a mere 150 river segments—puny compared to what has been lost.

The facts of river fatalities are startling. Entire river systems have fallen prey. The Tennessee River Valley has more miles of reservoir shoreline than surrounds all five Great Lakes. All but 149 miles of the 2,446 miles of the Missouri River have been dammed, and that 149 miles would have been, too, if it hadn't been included in the act in 1976.

The Colorado River basin has been impounded to such an extent that, with the exception of local floods, none of its water has reached the Pacific in decades. The Columbia has been reduced to a succession of reservoirs, with little or no moving water in between.

Almost all the free-flowing rivers of California's Sierras are shadows of their former selves. The magnificent stretch of Colorado's Upper Dolores River has been sacrificed in the name of irrigation water so expensive that no farmer can afford it. Glen Canyon, which has perhaps the most beautiful sandstone labyrinths in the world, now lies underneath Lake Powell, where you would need scuba equipment to enjoy it. And the list goes on.

How does this happen? The machinations by which dams are approved and funded is a textbook study in pork-barrel politics. Most water projects are approved on the basis of a highly theoretical study called "cost-benefit analysis." Its name sounds imposing, but the actual procedure is relatively simple.

The first step is an estimation of installation and operating costs of the project. Then the value of benefits is estimated from the goods and services that will be produced. Next are computed the secondary—or indirect—costs and benefits. For example, the direct benefits of a dam might include the revenues from the hydroelectric power it produces. The indirect benefit may be the estimated income from recreational activities on the flatwater, or lake, the dam creates.

The problem is that the procedure to conduct a "cost-benefit analysis" is considerably more subjective than one might believe, because decisions of what constitutes a cost or a benefit are not always straightforward.

Over the years this process of analysis has been criticized as reflecting the prejudices of the analyst. Since the agencies preparing the analysis are usually involved in construction, there is evidence that they are biased. The courts have found that they often either exaggerate benefits or underestimate costs in order to promote a dam.

The economic activity resulting from flatwater recreation, like water skiing, power boating, and fishing, are used to justify dams, but the lost potential revenues from river recreation, like whitewater rafting, kayaking, and canoeing, are commonly ignored. Often neglected are environmental damages, such as flooding of historic and archaeological sites, and consequences to fish and wildlife caused by changing water temperatures, increased salinity, and elimination of natural beaches.

Only recently has the science of ecology begun to rival that of engineering. Bill Thomas, author of *American Rivers: A Natural History*, maintains that, from a scientific standpoint, a dammed river is a polluted river, and that free-flowing streams are necessary to cleanse the environment:

The Congress and the public in general have yet to consider that every river, regardless of its location or size, is vitally important to the survival of man. Indicator warnings—fish kills, cancer scares, the decimation of pelicans and other creatures—hint that man's casual mistreatment of the river may indeed produce dire circumstances at some time in the future. And it is difficult to visualize the survival of man in a world with only poisoned water.

After all, cost-benefit analysis is economics, and it requires conversion of environmental damages into monetary terms. Dollar amounts must be placed on the environment as a measure of its value. But what price do you put on the aesthetic and ecological advantages of a free-flowing stream? Or their loss?

Perhaps the most intimidating player in the dam game is the Army Corps of Engineers. Dams alone are its driving force, as pointed out in *American Rivers: A Natural History*:

The Corps is not concerned with biological adversities. Instead it thinks of navigation and flood control; the rest be damned. Only in recent times has it given lip service to the environment, and only then to achieve public support for its own existence.

In the West, most dams are built by the Bureau of Reclamation, which has had its powers expanded from one of irrigation, so that it now operates some of the largest "cash-register" hydroelectric plants in the country, including Bonneville and Coulee dams on the Columbia River and Hoover and Glen Canyon dams on the Colorado River. The Tennessee Valley Authority, a major political force in the Southeast, has built some 50 dams throughout the river's basin. Many have proven to be economic disasters.

In his book, *A River No More*, Philip L. Fradkin puts the vested interests of dam builders into perspective:

> The power and the glory, not to mention the money, center around water and the means to convey it. Woe to any president who tries to cut back this system. It consists of ditches, flumes, penstocks, dams, canals, laterals, pipelines, aqueducts, and more ditches laid across how many tens of thousands of miles that bisect mountains, deserts, farmlands, and cities. It represents billions of dollars of water projects and a political system to procure them that has yet to be successfully thwarted.

Dams are often built so that development can move in, making another dam necessary to protect the development encouraged by the first, and so on. In his book *The River Killers*, Martin Heuvelmans explains how the Army Corps of Engineers perpetuates itself:

When an area is drained or a dam is built, "new" land is created, and it is soon crowded with people. These people demand greater protection from the very thing the Corps sought to alleviate. More pretentious projects are started which, in turn, attract more people. The cycle continues and grows more calamitous with each move.

The Cossatot River in the Ouachita Mountains of Arkansas is a good example. Gillham Dam was justified because of the flood damage it would prevent. Yet the area below the dam had nothing to protect: a few barns, a shack or two, a handful of gravel roads, and a pasture with several hundred head of cattle. (It would have been much cheaper to purchase the entire floodplain.) There had never been a flood death on the Cossatot. Nevertheless, the dam was built.

Hydroelectric benefits are claimed, even if the power isn't needed. The Alaska Power Authority proposed dams on the Susitna and other rivers, though it didn't have contracts with utility companies. The reason was simple: it was cheaper to use oil and gas. Dam developers receive not only cash subsidies, but also guaranteed markets for the power they produce. And it's no surprise that demand for electricity has been nowhere near what was projected.

Irrigation is often used to justify dams. Cheap water encourages agriculture, and the result is a substantial subsidy. Water that may have cost the government $70 to

$100 an acre-foot (the volume of water that would cover one acre of land one-foot deep) to develop is often sold for as little as $3 or $4 an acre-foot.

In the end, it may prove ironic that the most effective way of saving rivers is economics. If it can be shown that a project is inefficient, then the figures alone may stop the project. In his book *Stanislaus: The Struggle for a River*, Tim Palmer advises:

> Nowadays it takes more than righteousness and wilderness morality [to save a river]. It takes figures, ratios, tables. You want to fight a dam? Then you argue about diurnal temperature variation and dependable hydroelectric capacity. It's a war of statistics . . .

The year 1980 proved to be something of a watershed for the Wild and Scenic Rivers Act, with the largest number of rivers (26) added to the system in a single year, all of which were Alaskan. President Jimmy Carter, who made no friends with the dam lobby when he threatened to put the Army Corps of Engineers out of business, saw this as one of his greatest environmental achievements.

With the election of Ronald Reagan as president, it was feared that progress might be stalled on a riverless plateau. Some of that pessimism proved well-founded, but the Reagan administration was more amenable than expected—though not without some "gentle" prodding.

Numbers cannot tell the whole story, but a tally is revealing. In the first four years (1981 to 1984), not one river was added. Eventually 25 rivers were added, almost all in 1987.

With the Bush administration, things improved considerably. The number of river segments protected almost doubled, to the present total of 152. That brings the average to six new rivers to be protected every year since 1968.

In the twenty-five years since the ink dried on the act, there have been notable successes—over 10,000 miles of rivers saved. But much remains to be done. A long list of rivers has been identified by Congress as potential additions; but, as the past has proven, the process is slow. There are equally qualified rivers which haven't risen to the status of potential additions. *As a result, the rate of river mileage lost is 75 times greater than the rate of river preservation.*

The states that have solid, effective programs to protect rivers are in the minority. And even on state-protected rivers, the Federal Energy Regulatory Commission (FERC) can overrule the state's designation and issue dam permits, making it imperative that these rivers eventually be added to the federal system.

Meanwhile, several conservation groups are pursuing private pacts with federal agencies and corporations to buy some time. The Nature Conservancy has spent millions of dollars to purchase lands along rivers for preservation. The organization American Rivers has secured years of protection through agreements with the Forest Service and the forest-products industry.

Then there is the old-fashioned appeal to the grass roots, as occurred in the mid-sixties when Marble Gorge and Bridge Canyon dams were proposed for the Grand Canyon, prompting the Sierra Club to place full-page ads asking: "Should we flood the Sistine Chapel so tourists can get closer to the ceiling?" The response from the public, most of whom would never see the river, was so overwhelming that the politicians got the message and vetoed the project.

A dozen years later, another highly publicized debate arose over New Melones Dam on California's Stanislaus River. The controversy climaxed when river activist Mark Dubois chained himself to the riverbanks to stop further inundation. Preservation efforts were unsuccessful, but in the long run the river lobby won by bringing attention to both the misrepresentations of those profiting from the dam, and the importance of saving our last remaining rivers.

Reflecting on the work of the river conservation movement from the first major dam fight in 1913—when the famous naturalist John Muir opposed Hetch Hetchy Dam in Yosemite and lost—there have been victories; still, far too many rivers are irretrievably lost.

Undoubtedly, some dams do provide benefits which cannot be obtained in other ways: irrigation and domestic water supplies, flood control, hydroelectric power. But not all. Former Secretary of the Interior Cecil Andrus once argued in a conference in Idaho:

> Streams and rivers have other values than just for electric power generation and irrigation and transportation. We need free-flowing water left in the nation for many reasons—including the protection of certain forms of life, for recreation, for scenic values, for maintenance of the tenuous link between modern man and his natural world.

In *Time and the River Flowing*, François Leydet points out the dilemma:

> I suppose if we accept as a national policy that every resource of the country must be developed to the limit to support the greatest possible human population, then we should right now give up the fight to save any untouched vestiges of our natural heritage. All rivers must be dammed, to prevent their wasting water into the ocean, and the consequent destruction of the beauty of natural rivers must be shrugged off as one of the prices of progress.

If we decide, instead, that rivers are worth saving, then the political field must be leveled. Before another dam is built, its benefits should be proved so overwhelming that *no other reasonable alternative exists.* It is only right that the burden be placed on those who advocate change, not on those who support the status quo: a river in its natural state.

Otherwise, the consequences for all of us are too great to ignore because no force of nature affects the human spirit quite like running water. And, with few exceptions, no amount of progress can be worth the loss of a river flowing free.

ACKNOWLEDGMENTS

 Many people con-
tributed—often un-
knowingly—to *Whitewater Rafting*. Not all of them men-
tioned here. My thanks do not adequately express my debt
to them all.

A number of editors of the whitewater magazines—
Down River, River World, River Runner, and *Paddler*—
encouraged, or at least tolerated, my submissions over the
years, which gave me the foolhardy incentive to write further. Foremost among theses editors is Ken Hulick, who, in
the process, became a close friend as well.

I also appreciate the enthusiastic support of publisher Peter Burford for the project, as well as the fine editing skills of Lilly Golden.

The dozens of rafting companions with whom I have shared trips along the way have also been an inspiration. While there are too many to mention, my appreciation goes to them all.

And to the Nantahala Outdoor Center and its fine guides—and especially Janet Smith, Bunny Johns, and Payson Kennedy—I owe a special debt of gratitude for many unforgettable journeys.

My thanks also to my legal colleagues at Fulbright & Jaworski—in particular, Mike Steindorf and Hugh Hackney—for their enthusiastic support of a hobby that at times gets a little out of hand.

And last, but most important, I can never repay my parents for putting up with an endeavor that started twenty years ago when I was in college—a pursuit about which they worry still.

GLOSSARY

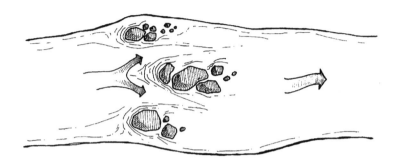

RIVER AND RAFTING TERMS

Catamaran raft A raft with two single tubes held together by a frame, providing the ultimate self-bailing craft

Cfs Cubic feet per second; a measurement of the volume of water flowing past a given point per second

Denier — A measurement commonly used to describe raft fabrics; the greater the denier, the coarser (and often stronger) the fabric

Draw stroke — Sideways pull of the paddle toward the raft

Drysuit — A nylon bodysuit with tightly fitting closures at wrists, ankles, and neck

Eddy — An area in the river where the current either stops or moves upstream—opposite the main current—usually found below obstructions and on the inside of bends

Eddy line — The sharp boundary between two currents of different velocity or direction, usually marked by swirling water and bubbles

Feather — Slight adjustments of an oar's blade to reduce the friction of water or air

Ferry A maneuver for moving a boat across the current, usually by rowing or paddling upstream at an angle

Frame The metal structure attached to rafts for the purpose of holding the oarlocks and for enabling gear to be secured above the floor of the raft

Gradient The slope of a riverbed, usually expressed in the number of feet per mile the river drops

Hole A reversal (see below)

Hypalon A fabric coating commonly used in raft manufacture

Hypothermia The serious medical condition caused by the lowering of body temperature, requiring immediate first aid

Lining Guiding the raft downstream from the shore with ropes to avoid running rapids

Neoprene   A fabric coating commonly used in raft manufacture

Oarhorns   The traditional U-shaped oarlock, often used because it allows the oars to be "feathered" and pulled into the raft

Portage   To carry boats and equipment around the rapids on shore

Put-in   The point of beginning a river trip

Pry stroke   Sideways push of the paddle away from the raft

Reversal   An area of the river where the current turns upstream and revolves back on itself, forming a treacherous current requiring caution; often called hydraulics, stoppers, keepers, curlers, and holes

Scout   To examine a rapid from shore

Standing wave	A high wave caused by the slowing of the current
Strainer	Exposed rocks, usually on the outside of a bend, presenting a hazard to boaters
Sweeper	Fallen trees or brush that lie in the path of the current
Thole pins with clips	An oarlock that holds the oar blade in a fixed position
Tongue	The smooth "V" of fast water found at the head of rapids, usually indicating the deepest and least obstructed channel
Wrapping	The partial submersion that occurs when a raft's upstream tube becomes lodged underwater against a boulder

INDEX